Tales From The Bench:
Essays On Life and Justice

Judge Sandra Arlene Simms (Ret.)

Pacific Raven Press Publishing, Hawai`i

First Edition: October, 2012
2nd Printing: January, 2013

Cover Design and Typesetting by Saforabu Graphix

Published by Pacific Raven Press Publishing
P.O. Box 678, Ka'a'awa, Hawai`i 96730
Email: pacificravenpress@gmail.com
Website: www.pacificravenpress.com
Telephone: 1-808-276-6864
Fax Number: 1-808-237-8974 USA

Published in the United States of America

This book is dedicated to my parents,
Gerald Raymond Nuckolls, Sr. (1921-2004)
and Vera Mae Nuckolls (1923-1991)

Table of Contents

Acknowledgements

I didn't start this project with the intention of writing a book; I merely was attempting to sort out some of my thoughts during a rather tumultuous time in my life. Writing was supposed to be a therapeutic endeavor, but as things often do, this therapy evolved into something else. I must thank my friend and my first reader, Michael Tanigawa, who enjoyed my recollections of family gatherings and believed my experiences were worth sharing with our diverse community. Michael also proved to be an invaluable resource, especially when he forwarded me copies of my files after a massive computer crash ate all of my writings. Because of him, I could not claim total destruction and end the project.

Then, Koreen Yogi's young son, Kyle Yogi, spoke through his mother, encouraging me to tell "my story." I also thank my colleague Ron Williams, who encouraged me to share my thoughts on law, justice and community for his *Mahogany* newspaper, which I began to do. When he published what I wrote, I began to think I was a writer! So, I continued. *Mahalo* ("thank you") to my secretary, Sharon Kato, and clerk, Susan Lum-Nagle, who emptied out a couple of file drawers containing all of my hand written trial notes and put them in boxes on my last day at court. They smiled and said, "Who knows what you can do with them…maybe this is a book." At quarterly lunch sessions, they still gave me pointers and read my work.

Then along came the incredible, visionary women of Pacific Raven Press, Ayin Adams and Kathryn Takara who insisted that "our stories be told" for future generations. With persistence and an almost missionary zeal, they extracted thoughts and emotions I had long ago buried, or so I thought. Thank you both. And I must express my gratitude to my brother David and his wife Claudia whose basement storage area housed my mom's entire humongous photo collection chronicling my every move from day one.

I send out a huge *mahalo* and much love to Hank and my children who lived it all, and endured our life stories all over again while I wrote. My gratitude also goes out to my Chicago *ohana* who has always had my back. I also want to acknowledge the late Bishop

Arthur Brazier and his wife Isabelle who continue to teach and inspire new generations.

Friends and colleagues who "urged" me on, keeping me inspired, include Daphne Barbee Wooten, Andre Wooten, Russ Barbee, Mike Healy, Lori Wada, Karen McKinnie, Jana Wolff, Myles Breiner, Bill Harrison, Eric Saks, Keith Shigetomi, Marsha McFadden, Dennis Anderson, RaeDeen Kurusada, Kathryn Xian, Link Patricia Russell McCloud, and Jerry and Marti Jones.

None of what I experienced would have occurred without the late Justice Yoshimi Hayashi and his colleagues on the inaugural Intermediate Court of Appeals, Judge Frank Padgett and Judge James S. Burns, who showed me and my family justice, humility and *aloha*.

Lastly, for making my random thoughts make sense to regular, non-legal people, I owe an incredible debt to my editor, Dr. Allison E. Francis. I am so grateful for all of you. *Mahalo.*

Introduction: Once Upon a Judge

On April 5, 2004, my father would have celebrated his 83rd birthday. Instead, it was the day of his "crossing over." Gerald Nuckolls, Sr. passed away in Chicago, Illinois. Suddenly, I remembered how I felt the day my mom died. When I received word of her death, I felt as if my life rug had been snapped from underneath me. My legs could not hold me up; my stomach had fallen out; a soaked sponge was wrung in my head. I was so scared for myself and for my family.

Now, what would happen if I had a problem? Who could I call? When my mother died, I thought, "How on earth would I measure up to being the rock my children could lean on as she had been for me?" I was scared then, but now with the death of my father, I felt true fear. I no longer had parents. Unmistakably, I was now the parent.

On the Sunday prior to my father's death, I had just returned from a "Science for Judges" conference in New York, and was collecting my baggage at the Honolulu airport when my cell phone rang. My brother David was calling because our father was being admitted to the hospital. But I was jet lagged, edgy, and distracted, so I didn't process David's words clearly. I had too many things on my mind. For one, I was concerned about whether I would even be appointed again since my term as judge was up, and my re-appointment was in jeopardy. Secondly, my husband Hank was still recovering from complications to his cancer treatment, and my son Richard, was in even deeper trouble with the police. Not surprisingly, the media dogs were circling hungrily. So, despite the temporary uplifting energy I experienced from my colleagues at the conference, my life appeared to be crumbling around me. Nevertheless, I maintained a stoic front.

In actuality, I was falling apart. Few of my relatives and close friends knew of my crisis, but those who did or suspected how fragile I was, didn't dare speak of it. How did I get to this stage in my professional and personal life?

Beginnings

I was born in Chicago, Illinois. I was a graduate of Hyde Park High School, and then obtained a B. A. from the University of Illinois,

Chicago with a major in Sociology and Political Science. After graduating from the University of Illinois, I temporarily opted for the glamorous life, so I became a flight attendant for United Airlines from 1972-1977. In this position, I met and married my husband, Hank.

Inspired by the civil rights movements, I began to pursue a career in law and earned my Juris Doctor degree from DePaul University, College of Law in 1978. Not surprisingly, when Hank and I moved to Hawai`i in 1979, lots of miles were burned between Honolulu and Chicago. Since Hank worked for United Airlines, this was not such a big deal, except when we endured the nine hour flight with our two infants, Sharon and Richard. They travel well now.

My parents visited us in Hawai`i often, so our children had a strong bond with their grandparents. Our first-born, Sharon, in particular, was treated quite queenly by them since she was the first grandchild. But after my mom died in 1991, we did not see my father as much.

During this transitional time on my home front, much had and was occurring in my professional life. From 1980 until March, 1982, I clerked for the Honorable Yoshimi Hayashi, then Chief Judge for the newly formed Intermediate Court of Appeals. Two years later, I served as Deputy Corporation Counsel for the City and County of Honolulu from 1982 until 1991, where I worked as legal counsel to a variety of city agencies and commissions, including the Police Commission, Civil Service Commission, Liquor Commission, Building, Public Works, Fire Department, and Family Support Division. Also, I was a Staff Attorney for the Department of the Attorney General's Office of Information Practices. These were exciting yet exhausting times for me and my family.

In those years after we moved to Hawai`i, my father's church, The Apostolic Church of God in Chicago, grew massively into the powerful and influential church it is today. My dad was a steadfast and integral part of its growth, chairing its Deacon Board and Board of Trustees. By that time, my father had remarried, and spent time building a nice life with his new wife, Wilhelmina Moore.

In November of 1991, I made history by becoming the first African American female judge appointed in the State of Hawai`i by Chief

Justice Herman Lum to the District Court of the First Circuit. A few years later in 1994, I was appointed by Governor John Waihe`e to the position of Circuit Court Judge for the First Judicial Circuit, State of Hawai`i. As a trial judge, I have presided over matters involving domestic violence, restraining orders, civil proceedings and felony jury trials, a substantial number of which were extensively covered by the media.

Fortunately, my father was able to celebrate most of my life's achievements with me despite the ocean that flowed between us. Never was a father prouder of his daughter than when he knew I had taken my oath as judge.

Transitions

April, 2004. Now I was at another major transition in my life. My father, my husband, my son and my career appeared to be convening at a major crossroads. What could and would I do? Despite the crises that appeared to overwhelm me on that fateful day when David called to tell me the news about our father, I knew instinctively that all was going to be well because the spirits of my parents and grandfather were, and continue to, surround me. So, no matter what final decision might arise from the Judicial Selection Committee, I knew what I had to do: love my family, honor my profession, and appreciate my life.

This book then, is my labor of love. Here, I share intriguing cases, life lessons, and incredible transitions and transformations I have both witnessed and experienced. It is from my beginnings in Chicago and professional achievements in Hawai`i that I draw these tales from the bench.

Chapter 1

How to Get Out of Jury Duty

In one of my first criminal jury trials where I was the presiding judge, an experienced defense lawyer, Mike Healy, was defending an African American client. During jury selection, he launched into what was a normal, well-rehearsed routine designed to discern whether potential jurors held any prejudicial feelings toward his Black client.

"Looking at my client, can you believe him to be innocent of the charge against him?" he asked the group of 30 or so potential jurors. "Does the fact that he is African-American make it less likely to see him as innocent?" He continued probing for signs of bias. He then challenged the jury panel to look around the room. As the confused jurors began self-consciously looking around, with a dramatic flourish, Mr. Healy announced, "THERE ARE NO OTHER BLACK PEOPLE IN THE ROOM!"

As he spoke, several of them glanced at me quizzically. I just smiled and shrugged in mock horror. After seeing my ease, the potential jurors began smiling at Mr. Healy whose back was to me as he addressed them. In an instant, he caught himself and turned to look at me with an embarrassed smile. He recovered quickly and said, "There are no other Black people in the room except for her Honor, of course." We all had a good laugh which broke the tension. Quickly, the potential jurors assured counsel and me that they harbored no such prejudices and would make their decision based on the law and facts, not race. The trial continued.

I share this incident because many people continue to believe that our justice system is not only biased against Blacks, but that there is no Black presence in the courtroom, except for the stereotypical Black defendant. Indeed, in Hawai`i there are only a few Black police officers, prosecutors, and defense lawyers. African Americans make up less than 3% of the state's population. Our Afro American Lawyers Association, established in 1988, still cannot summon more than a handful of attorneys to hold a meeting. Even though times have changed since the mid-20th century, many of my colleagues in the legal system aren't disavowed of this lack. Defense lawyers like Mike Healy feel compelled to go to extremes, even using histrionics in their attempt to approve a jury panel that can be racially fair. Even they often are distrustful of our system's ability to fairly adjudicate Blacks and other minority defendants, as this example and countless others I saw in those years on the bench showed.

So, since this tradition of the underrepresentation of African Americans on the other side of the bench was always a bit unnerving, I found it disconcerting when many of my well-meaning Black friends and acquaintances seized upon the historical significance of my appointment as giving them an inside track on how to get "out" of jury duty. After expressing their momentary pride or awe at my status, they would pull me aside for "advice."

"Girl, I just got this summons for jury duty and I do not want to go down there. I just don't have time for this, I am so busy." Or, "Hey judge, you know the ropes; how can I get out of this . . . I just can't be bothered."

Well, it bothered me too, but not for the same reasons. Quite frankly, their request for advice still bothers me.

Why? Well, let us just look at the facts. Daily reports out of programs like "The Innocence Project" tell of defendants being exonerated after years spent in prisons around the country when new scientific evidence reveals their innocence. The overwhelming majority of these defendants were Black and almost every single one of the exonerated Black defendants had been convicted by an all-white jury. The fact is that historically, African Americans and other minorities have been systematically excluded from the selection process.

For example, Dr. RaeDeen Keahiolalo-Karasuda, a Senior Research Associate at Kamehameha Schools, wrote her Ph.D. dissertation on the disproportionate representation of native Hawaiians in Hawai`i prisons, after an inmate pointed out that during roll call at Halawa Prison, names beginning with the letter "K," which is the most common letter of Hawaiian surnames, took up more than half of the daily roster.

I'm not suggesting that having African Americans (or any other minorities) on a jury suddenly will result in mass acquittals of Black defendants. However, when there is diversity on the jury panel, folks are much more inclined to leave their prejudices at the door. This bears true not just for Blacks, but for other ethnic minorities as well. And this is especially true in Hawai`i where native Hawaiians, people of Samoan heritage and to some extent, Filipino heritage, are disproportionally represented in the criminal justice system.

When a jury panel is diverse, a convicted defendant is much more likely to have been judged solely on the evidence presented rather than on some deep-seated, or shallow prejudice that "he's Black," or "Hawaiian," or "Other." Nevertheless, diversity on the jury is a huge step in the right direction to assure fairness in our judicial system.

The Underrepresented Minority

Jury studies have shown that in many jurisdictions in the United States, Blacks are systematically excluded from jury pools. In most instances, they are not counted, or included in the populations from which jurors are drawn. Even when Blacks and other minorities are included in the jury pool, the likelihood that they are selected by the attorneys can be reduced by the use of peremptory challenges. Peremptory challenges allow a juror to be dismissed for no reason. It is the primary way in which Blacks, in particular, were excluded from juries, especially in many of our southern states, until the US Supreme Court decided a case in 1971, called *Batson v the United States*. In that case, the court ruled that the use of peremptory challenges exercised only against minorities could be opposed. Our Hawai`i Supreme Court took it one step further and ruled in a similarly titled case, *State of Hawai`i v. Batson* (1990) that *anytime* a peremptory challenge was used against a juror of the same ethnicity as the defendant, then a presumption of prejudice arose and attorneys had to give a non-racial reason for the exclusion.

So, my standard response to "friendly" requests for opting out of jury duty eventually evolved into a mini-lecture, or a rant, on the importance of jury duty and the need for Black folks to be a part of this decision-making process. Could they not realize how important their service would be in assuring fairness in our legal system? I still wonder how African Americans could complain about the prejudice in our legal system, then turn around and complain about jury duty. Not surprisingly, after a short while, people stopped asking me how to get out of jury duty.

I know that our criminal justice system is not perfect; indeed, it has many flaws and a painful history of racial inequities. Yet, I still fervently believe the jury system remains a far better means of determining guilt or innocence than any other process. In our country, a defendant charged with a crime need not prove he or she is innocent. Our justice system demands that the State, which is the prosecution, bring concrete evidence of a defendant's guilt and prove it beyond a reasonable doubt.

When a charge is brought forward, the State then is required to summon its formidable resources and, indeed, they are formidable to secure a conviction. The State, or prosecution, can call on the police for statements, and issue subpoenas commanding the presence of witnesses, with serious consequences for non-compliance. The State has access to extensive crime labs and specialists, much like those seen on television programs like "CSI." The State has access to expert witnesses who can be summoned to speak on any topic imaginable. Consequently, the prosecution knows how to try a case, using all these formidable resources in presenting its evidence to the twelve citizens who comprise the jury—the same jury who will decide whether that high standard of proof, "beyond a reasonable doubt," has been met.

In criminal cases, all twelve jurors *must* agree and their decision *must* be unanimous. Of course, simply having a Black person on the jury, or even as the judge, does not present the defendant with a "get out of jail free" card, nor will all Black defendants instantly receive an acquittal. However, a diverse panel of jurors usually means that the evidence and the law will be filtered through the lens of a variety of life experiences.

Getting back to Mike Healy, we've talked and laughed about his outburst in court since that day. But the point is that he only wanted to insure that his client had the best defense and an unbiased jury. Unfortunately, he also knew that historically, in courts both in Hawai`i and the mainland, Black jurors were, and are rarely seen. For these reasons, he wanted the potential jurors to in essence, "examine themselves" for any vestiges of unconscious prejudice towards a Black defendant. Why? Because we know that racism in the legal system does exist. Prejudices still exist. If a potential juror knows nothing of African Americans save for the "Willie Horton" distortions promulgated by media, then every defense attorney, representing a Black client has to ask these uncomfortable questions. Jurors may squirm and look uneasy, and I understand that.

Unfortunately, Mike Healy's bluntly posed questions were necessary, and such inquiries regarding racial profiling continue to be necessary. Race continues to be the "elephant in the room" in our criminal justice system and in our nation. Period.

Indeed, once while I was conferring with the attorneys in a case during jury selection, a potential juror approached the bench and asked to be excused from the panel because, he said, "I do not like Black people." Since the defendant on trial was not Black, nor were any of the attorneys, I assumed he meant me! I assured him that liking me had nothing to do with the decision he would be called upon to make about the defendant. I did not need to be liked, so I declined to excuse him from jury duty. Both attorneys were offended at his request and when, oddly enough, he was actually called into the pool, neither attorney asked him any questions. He was blatantly ignored while he sat in the jury box, awaiting his turn to be questioned. At the end of the day, he was unceremoniously and peremptorily bumped from duty. I almost felt sorry for him as he sat uncomfortably throughout the day's selection process as other jurors saw him receiving "the silent treatment."

Since then, I have thought of that potential juror and wondered what emboldened him to approach me and the other attorneys who were also non-Caucasian with such a provocative declaration. What did he really think I would do? Slink from his stare and excuse him, declare a recess and run from the room, or apologize for my Blackness? Today, I still wonder what prompts us to such acts of prejudice. Hopefully, spending a day observing the lengths we go to assure fair trials had an impact on his views.

The Selection Process

Jurors in Hawai`i are drawn from a variety of sources, but the registrar of voters is the prime source. Each year, the Jury Pool Office sends out thousands of questionnaires to randomly selected citizens whose names are then placed in a jury pool. As cases come up for trial, groups of jurors are summoned to report for jury duty. The jury pool in a given case can range from as few as 30 people to hundreds (in cases with high publicity and/or issues of sexual assault, murder and so forth). In the end, twelve people are selected—twelve people whom the court deems can be fair—to listen to the evidence, and make their decision solely on the evidence and the law that applies to it.

Contrary to popular thought, jurors do not resolve to be ignorant couch potatoes, or empty of opinions about the issues facing our society. On that day, they just need to make their decision about the defendant before them based solely on the evidence and the law. That's all.

When a trial ends, most judges will take time to sit down in an informal session with jurors to answer questions or as we say in Hawai`i, "talk story." I know I always did. It's one of the more rewarding aspects of the position. These "talk story" sessions serve as a de-briefing, especially in trials involving graphic violence, high publicity, or tense familial, emotional situations. The first question jurors would invariably ask me was whether their decision was "right." I would always assure them that the decision they made was the right one because it was based on the evidence they actually received, not what a "CSI," or "Law and Order" television episode suggested was the proper outcome.

Jurors invariably asked what I would have decided, so I would assure them that my decision was irrelevant – especially since I was the one who had decided what evidence they would hear. Jurors were always interested in whether a defendant had a prior record, or what kind of sentence a convicted defendant would be facing. I would answer them. And, in this informal setting, I would always invite them to attend the sentencing when a defendant was found guilty.

Jurors often were curious about whether a convicted person would try to contact them, to which my answer was always a resounding "No," except once. In this case, the swift response of the late Honolulu Police Department (HPD) Chief Michael Nakamura literally saved the day. The defendant had been charged with non-violent gun possession charges and made the decision to go to trial "pro se," which means without an attorney to represent him. In felony criminal cases, this is hardly ever a wise decision. The jury eventually convicted the defendant of all the charges, but he was still out on bail pending sentence.

What he did next seems unbelievable to most of us. Even though he did not have access to the personal information of the jurors, he had one juror's name, so he found her contact information in the phone book, then called her, much to her surprise! Had he elected to proceed to trial with an attorney, his attorney would have assuredly advised him against this course of action and its serious consequences.

The juror he called just happened to be the chief of staff for one of our congressional members, so she immediately knew she should contact me. I actually advise jurors that in the unlikely event that they were inappropriately contacted by a defendant, they should call me directly—precisely what this juror did. Nevertheless, I was taken aback by this turn of events. This had never happened to me before, nor to any of the judges I polled quickly. There was no precedent for such behavior here.

So, I immediately contacted Chief Nakamura who was right on task, asking for the names, numbers, and addresses of every juror on that case. Then he dispatched an officer to each of them! Of course, the defendant also received a surprise visit from the police as well. The defendant actually was quite apologetic, belatedly realizing the impact of his action.

So, when Black folks, or anyone else for that matter, ask me how to get out of jury duty my answer is: DON'T! Since African Americans and other underrepresented minorities are conspicuously absent from the jury process, their involvement is desperately needed. Their presence, in no small way, balances out the harmful tradition of racial inequity still in existence in our justice system. All jurors, regardless of ethnicity or gender, have a critical, vital role in the preservation of our constitutional liberties, and to insure that justice is served. When the law and evidence is filtered through the lens of a diverse jury panel whose members still are able to agree on guilt or innocence – that is justice! Jury duty is service to your community and your state, so you have to be there.

Moreover, those of us actively within the system must find ways to make jury service possible and palatable. For example, we can create accommodations in the scheduling to assure that jurors can leave in time to pick up children from day care, or call for a later trial start for jurors who don't work 9-5. Perhaps we can even figure out a way to work around a juror's scheduled doctor's appointment. Most judges are not averse to setting up these accommodations because they are not impossible to do. Therefore, we should not put up roadblocks in the path of jury duty, nor should we maintain the continued exclusion of Blacks and other minorities in the system.

I am absolutely convinced that when twelve people of varied age, income, occupation, life experience, and yes, race, can all agree on a defendant's guilt or innocence, then, here is justice, in its purest form, as intended by our Constitution. It is as simple and as complicated as that. So, next time you consider how best to be released from jury service, don't! Just consider how you can contribute to keeping our system honest – and to making us all accountable.

Chapter 2

Women and Broken Trust

Most criminal defendants are males under the age of 35. A significant number of their victims are women. Not surprisingly, women are the primary victims of sexual assaults, acts of domestic violence, and trafficking. In this chapter, I remember some of the more vulnerable situations where I witnessed women victimized or entrapped by those they trusted most. It is my intent that from this vantage point, these tales will raise awareness and suggest ways in which we as a community, and not just the legal system, can empower women and ourselves.

Domestic violence clearly remains a most serious issue. In my years on the bench, we saw a rash of cases that ended in unspeakably horrific acts, always to the detriment of the woman involved. I don't want to minimize this point; however, I would be remiss if I overlooked the uncomfortable fact that violence directed at women and girls is as old as humankind. Historically, women have seldom been seen as equal partners in any given society and violence directed at them raised little alarm. Indeed, in some eras of our own American history, women were enslaved, bred, deemed incapable of having basic rights, and treated like property.

As the modern women's movement has strengthened, we have come to recognize and refuse to tolerate violence against women and girls as a societal norm, and rightly so. I am of the belief that criminal prosecution of violent acts directed against women is proper and necessary, but sadly, in some circles, this is not a norm. There are still pockets of society desperately clinging to the notion that a man is entitled to control a female in a relationship because some men still think, "she must do as I say or else."

This belief was all too apparent in a case involving a man we will call Brian and his girlfriend Trina[1]. Brian and Trina were a young, attractive couple who both came from upper middle class, professional families. Brian owned his own business while Trina attended college and worked part time. They both lived with their parents. Nevertheless, their relationship was tumultuous, to say the

---

[1] I will be using pseudonyms to protect both parties involved in all the case studies referenced in this book.

least. Unfortunately, they had a child. Brian thought this would be the thing to heal their relationship and for a time it appeared to do so, but Brian and Trina were not married nor living together, despite her family's recommendation that she do so.

Nor did Trina file a paternity action in order to secure child support payments for her son because Trina relied on her and Brian's respective abilities to be civil and reasonable people. They set up their own visitation schedule and Brian gave her money, on occasion, but not very often. Trina's parents were not pleased with the relationship, or with Brian's increasingly erratic behavior. He became more and more demanding of Trina and their son's time. When he did not get his way, he just stopped giving Trina any support at all. Trina broke off with him, so Brian came to her work site bearing roses and chocolates. They made up.

But rifts and reunions happened, again and again and again. He called her every day, at work, at home and would sometimes be seen by her relatives and friends following her in his car. Or, Brian would just show up unannounced and demand new conditions for their relationship, changes in the schedule, and new amounts of money to be paid. He was starting to stalk her. Trina's parents grew more frustrated and angry, but held their tongues because of their concern for their grandson.

Begrudgingly, Trina's family tolerated Brian's comings and goings until things changed for the worse. Trina had once again broken up with Brian and emphatically declared this would be the last time. This time, she said, she simply did not love him anymore. Plus, he had provided no support for the son he claimed to love so much. So with her parents' help, she finally filed for paternity and a temporary restraining order (TRO) barring Brian from harassing her and coming in contact with her.

We now know that the most dangerous time in these types of relationships occurs when the woman finally decides to end it. Unfortunately for Brian and Trina, this proven dynamic was not as widely understood as it is now. Trina was now in real danger.

One fateful morning, Trina dropped her son off with the sitter before heading to her college classes. Brian had pulled up behind her car in the sitter's parking stall of the "secured" apartment complex. He had been able to gain entry because one of his family members lived in the same complex. He told Trina he just wanted to hug his son because he had not seen him in a while because of the restraining order she had filed. Since he was tugging on her heartstrings, Trina relented and allowed Brian to hug the boy before she took him inside to the sitter.

But when she came back to her car, Brian was still there. He wanted to "talk." Instead of initiating a conversation, he threatened her with a 12 inch kitchen knife, covered her mouth and yanked her into his car. Holding the knife at her stomach he declared, "You'll talk to me now!" He drove the short distance to his family's parking stall, keeping the knife at her stomach while his free hand steered the wheel. He parked the car and dragged her out even though Trina desperately was struggling to escape.

Fortuitously, a passerby heard the yelling, and turned towards them, but Brian discreetly held the knife out of view. In that instant, Trina was able to break free, and ran toward the complex's guard shack yelling to the guard to call the police because her boyfriend had a knife and was threatening to kill her. The young, startled guard went to make the call as Brian strolled in calmly and nonchalantly. He patiently told the inexperienced guard to ignore Trina because "she's crazy" and that there was "no problem." "Yes, there is a problem!" Trina screamed, as the guard looked from Trina to Brian, trying to figure out what was going on. In a monstrous instant, Brian pulled out the knife, grabbed Trina and demanded that the guard call Brian's uncle instead.

Luckily, a second security guard outside the shack during the exchange heard everything, so he immediately called 911. The police already were responding with blaring sirens and drawn guns. Eerily, this was a quiet, late morning and hardly anyone was out on the streets of this upscale suburban complex. Yet, despite the arrival of the police, Brian refused to drop the knife.

Finally, after several entreaties by the officers who were poised to pull the triggers on their nine millimeters, Brian put down the knife and was arrested immediately. Trina collapsed in relief. When they searched Brian's car, the police located a clothesline rope. Had it not been for the second security guard's immediate actions this tale might have ended quite differently; Trina could have been killed or seriously wounded.

In the end, Brian was charged with a series of felony counts, including kidnapping and terroristic threatening. Undaunted and confident, he demanded a trial. Brian believed that the charm and beguile he had been using for years on Trina would work on the jury as well. He sat confidently, feigning shock as Trina described the incidents of that day. After the prosecution presented its evidence, Brian elected to testify in court, which is a highly unusual maneuver in criminal trials.

When he took the stand, he spoke directly to the jurors, presenting himself at his most charming and engaging. Trina's parents watched in horror from the gallery as he began his version of the events. He told the assembled jurors that he had no plans to kill Trina that day because he actually planned to kill himself since he loved and missed her so much. He said that he just needed to exchange a few last words with her before he committed suicide. What about the knife? Brian calmly explained that he pulled the knife on Trina to show how sincere he was about his love for her. Just like Romeo, he was prepared to take his own life if he could not have her. She had to understand this.

Moreover, he denied that the knife was pointed at her stomach, explaining that he had actually held the knife to his own throat! Trina was making this stuff up! So, how does he explain the rope? Well, he was not carrying the rope to use on Trina; he brought it so he could rig it to the door and kill himself, in the event some good Samaritan tried to thwart his suicide plans. He calmly explained that while he was upset that his relationship with Trina had soured, hell, he also was upset at his business partners, too. They, like everyone else, were swindling him out of his money. Even though Brian lived to tell the court his tale of misery and woe, the jury didn't buy his Shakespearean heroics. They found him guilty.

Brian and Trina's tale reminds us of the universality of domestic violence because no race, no ethnicity, no economic level, no education level, no social status assures immunity from its devastating effects on people, especially in this case.

Fatal Desires

But at other times, one woman's desire to feel wanted and attractive can create a different kind of vulnerability. Take Carly. Slim and attractive, she looked younger than the fifty years she had actually lived. Younger men, particularly teenage boys, made her feel desirable, attractive and young. Carly lavished gifts on these young men, allowing them to use her home as a hang-out, feeding them food, and supplying them with the latest video games. Some of these boys even had free use of her body. Perhaps she saw herself as a hip, mature woman, providing teenagers with an exciting, even sexy place to relax and chill out, but this did not work out well for her because she seemed to choose violent, abusive young men. This would result, sadly, in her violent death at the hands of one teenage sociopath.

For Carly, staying young meant dressing young, and acting young and what some would call "foolish." She bought the media's obsession with eternal youth, eschewing the staid, middle class, middle-aged matron's life she had left behind on the mainland. In Hawai`i, Carly was a new woman, befriending Waikīkī's "stray" youth, mostly boys, until one day, these teenagers embodied their juvenile delinquency. Their lead *gangsta*, Puck, came up with a scheme to rob and kill her, telling the other young boys that she had "dissed" or disrespected him. She had made the mistake of calling him her "bitch boy" in front of her friends, so in retaliation he sold his "homies" on "the plan."

While the other boys sat in the next room recklessly playing video games, he brutally stabbed Carly to death in her bedroom. When the teen gamers became aware of the brutal crime enacted just a few feet from where they sat joking and snacking on *"pupus"* or snacks, their macho bravado dissolved into primal fear and gut-wrenching guilt. The traumatized boys immediately told their parents what had occurred, despite threats from Puck that he would have them killed for "snitching." Without delay, these parents marched their boys to the police.

Sadly, Carly had just wanted to feel loved, so she offered herself to young boys, thinking this would be the best route to her definition of happiness. For Carly, this meant that to be loved you must look younger, thinner...hipper...dead.

During the trial, watching Carly's mainland family members was painful. How sad that they knew so little about her and the disconcerting life she had created after she arrived in Hawai`i. As the evidence unfolded, I watched shock and pain wash across their faces. I was relieved when, just before the grisly evidence photos of her sprawled and bloodied on her bed were to be presented to the jury, my assistant Sharon had the presence of mind to quietly approach Carly's family and discreetly escort them outside the courtroom during the viewing. Her misguided quest for youth and acceptance had led to her brutal death.

Although Carly's story truly was distressing, I must say that some of the most heart-wrenching incidents of domestic violence I witnessed as a judge in Hawai`i involved young girls who were abused and sexually assaulted by the men they trusted the most: boyfriends, husbands, family members and yes, even teachers. Sadly, sometimes these young girls are let down the hardest by other women to whom they turned to for support, or worst yet, their friends and family simply did not believe them. Fortunately, as we have learned more about the dynamics of abuse, most of us now know that trust can be breached by family and friends, but this understanding has evolved slowly. Denial was, and still is, big on both sides of the trust equation.

Special Treatment

Take the case of Cherie. She was one of six children in her family. Cherie's parents owned a small family food business where everyone worked except her. Instead, Cherie was singled out early by her father to receive "special treatment." Her father forced her to have sexual intercourse with him from the age of thirteen until she was nearly twenty years old. Tragically, her own father raped her repeatedly for over five years. When Cherie attempted to refuse her father's advances, he threatened her, before saying he only raped her for "her own good, to "prepare her for marriage." Destroying the family unity further, he told Cherie that her mother's physical appearance was not enough to keep him aroused. Sick stuff, indeed.

Finally, Cherie confided the abuse to a friend, who confronted Cherie's father. Cherie's father punched her friend out, sending him to the hospital with serious injuries. Needless to say, when Cherie's friend brought assault charges against the father, all hell broke loose. Now that the family secret was out, her father's carefully constructed veneers were brutally and irrevocably shattered as the truth evolved. I say evolved because it took time for Cherie's family to accept the truth.

When Cherie tried to tell her mother what had been taking place, her mother called her a liar. Cherie's sisters and brothers, unfortunately, blamed Cherie for creating chaos in the family. So, by the time the matter came to court for sentencing on the sexual assault charges, Cherie was a mental health disaster. She no longer lived with her family and had undergone months of therapy. In the courtroom she sat away from them, flanked by victim counselors.

Despite the 80 degree temperatures outside, Cherie was dressed in grotesquely over-sized, rolled up sweatpants and a huge hooded jacket that completely covered her head and face. Clearly, she wore nothing that would hint at her physical attractiveness.

During the hearing, testimony was presented to me by both sides urging their respective remedies. The State wanted a ten year jail term while Cherie's father's attorney urged probation. Cheri's mother, her sisters and other family members begged me to spare him a jail term. Her siblings then sneered while Cherie described her years of torment to a room full of strangers who cared more about her than her actual family members. This was a sad case since no one was free from suffering. I ruled in favor of the State because in this matter, the jail term was appropriate.

When sexual assault involves very young children it is a difficult and heart-wrenching experience. Nothing tears the soul more than the spectre of babies and kindergarteners as sexual assault victims. We can't handle it. That there are people who would sexually assault children is horrible enough, but when a family member is involved, the confusion and pain is excruciating. Sometimes, even parents are unwilling to believe their own children because it is too difficult to think that familial trust would be broken. For some people, it is easier to live in denial, especially when the accused family member assures you that nothing happened at first. Of course, some children make things up, or mimic and repeat things they've heard grown folks say. But when such terrible accusations turn out to be the truth, nothing is more rupturing to the family dynamic. Even death is easier to deal with because it's a normal part of life. Sexual assault on children is not.

Mommy, It Hurts

Picture this: a mother is bathing her six year old daughter just before bed when the girl announces that she does not like Uncle Sid because he keeps touching her "down there" and "now it hurts." Mom is stunned and shaking as the words send chills, rage and earth-shattering tremors throughout her body in the now spinning bathroom. Then the child says, "He does it to Samantha too," in that matter-of-fact voice that six year olds have. By now, the mother is visibly shaking and trying to hold back the scream rising from deep within, but she needs to preserve a veneer of calm so she can get more information from her daughter, despite the sickening, sinking horror she feels.

Steeling her emotions, she finishes the bath and dresses her child for bed. She collapses as she recounts the horror to her husband who is even more shaken. Uncle Sid is his *brother!* Uncle Sid lives downstairs with *their* mother. Samantha, his other niece, lives in the back cottage - *with his wife's sister!* To complicate this sad situation even more, all of the family members live in and contribute financially to the same homestead.

And with that revelation, spoken by a six year old innocent, a family is ripped apart by sexual violence. Two little girls are now thrust in the center of a family drama from which no one will ever be the same.

The unfortunate truth about any type of domestic abuse is that the family honor is at stake. You have all lived in the same house, shared meals, and family celebrations. You have laughed together and cried together, but now the life and home you all share is divided and crumbling. Suddenly, every family member feels obligated to take a side, which might ultimately devolve into a sick game between dire opponents rather than a strategic resolution amongst a loving family unit.

Strangers from the courts, the law, the medical arenas, are now barging in, asking questions, demanding answers, looking for evidence and staking out positions. Police officers, psychiatrists, and attorneys all claim to vindicate the accusing mother, with her six year old child at the center. Other young siblings and playmates are questioned, but they never "saw" Uncle Sid do those horrible things to the girls. Obviously, this does not mean that it didn't happen; it just means that they did not witness any inappropriate touching. But, their ignorance suddenly puts them on the "other side" of this tragic game, so these children can't play together anymore, nor can they watch cartoons together or share after school snacks with grandma.

Tragically, it turns out, the sexual abuse had been occurring for months. Disturbing psychiatric evaluations revealed that Uncle Sid sat around the children's play table with his fingers thrust into the girls' vaginas. Soon, other children began to recall little things that went unnoticed at the time, while others steadfastly insisted they never saw or experienced anything. We now know that Uncle Sid is a pedophile and that this is how they operate – as the charming, kind, and considerate man who carefully eases his way into constant contact with young children, under the unsuspecting eyes of the children's protectors.

When this case went to trial, the entire extended family—children, aunties, uncles, mothers and grandmothers— was in the courtroom, representing both sides. And, for the umpteenth time, the little girls had to wrench out the details of Uncle Sid's horrific violations.

"It was burning and itching," the young girl told her mother, the police, the psychiatrist, then the doctor, and now me, the judge, and a room full of complete strangers, as well as some disbelieving family members. "He kept digging in there," this six year old child told the doctor, who examined her, diagnosing a urinary tract infection. Upsettingly enough, each day the stricken family members left the same homestead, and headed to trial in separate vehicles to sit on opposite sides of the courtroom. This could have been a wedding gathering, except that instead of a benevolent minister nodding happily to both the bride and groom's families, I was the judge, eyeing a ruptured family with the prosecutor's people sitting in high agitation on the right, and the defense's people sitting in stony silence on the left. Instead of sharing smiles, no one in this family looked at each other. Mom, Dad, auntie, the girls, replayed the terrifying and sick scenes again and again. The police testified, then the psychiatrist, and even, Uncle Sid. Here truly was a courtroom filled with pain. No one was undamaged by these events. Uncle Sid was convicted by the jury and served time.

In the years since I've left the bench, my awareness of the vulnerability of women and girls in our society who are victims of domestic and sexual violence, has been magnified exponentially. In Hawai`i, I have had the privilege of being a part of groups like the Soroptimist International of Waikīkī, part of an international service organization whose goals are to improve the lives of women and girls around the world. Kathryn Xian's "GirlFest Hawai`i" on O`ahu has done much to raise this community's understanding of the impact of violence directed against women and girls. The work of other organizations like the Domestic Violence Action Center, and Pacific Alliance Against Slavery, continue to raise our consciousness and compassion for everyone who has suffered from direct or indirect domestic and sexual abuse.

Chapter 3

Through the Eyes of the Judge

Trial judges hear and see things you could never have imagined, especially on the criminal docket. The nightly news and its thirty second sound bites can't begin to scratch the surface of the scope of the stuff you experience in criminal court. The criminal docket takes those of us in the justice system, into another world, an almost surreal universe where we are called upon to truly suspend all judgment. Simultaneously, we try to comprehend some of the most incomprehensible situations humans can engage in, with some measure of empathy and understanding. While you may not have shared similar experiences with those who appear before you at the bench, criminal court is probably the one place that demands, at the very least, some form of situational diversity.

Why does diversity matter, you might say, especially since a crime is a crime? I wish it could be so simple, but unfortunately it is not. Minorities are still grossly overrepresented in our criminal justice system and try as we might, that is not going to change any time soon. In Hawai`i courts for instance, underrepresented minorities, African Americans, Samoans, Filipinos, and sadly, Native Hawaiians, are disproportionately represented in criminal proceedings.

And, while it may be easy to simply overlook these anomalies by hiding behind an ostensibly soothing but misguided belief that underrepresented minorities are predisposed to commit crime, the somber truth is that our society simply is unable to confront the elephant in the room of race. And in the criminal justice system, the elephant stands firmly in the doorway of the courthouse. Our nation's prisons hold widely disproportionate numbers of Blacks and Hispanic males and nearly 1/3 of Black males under the age of 35 have some involvement with criminal proceedings. We wrestle to find ways to assure ourselves that racial profiling is not about race, when it simply is.

Electing an African American president is, of course, a tremendously significant milestone and may signal that some of our racial woes are over. However, be assured that all is not well, yet. Visions of post-racial America vanish at the door to the criminal courts in our country, and even here in Hawai`i. Nevertheless, trial judges have the unique challenge of impacting the lives of the people who stand before them and view that challenge solemnly. We also must approach these challenges with detachment and objectivity.

Detachment. Objectivity. The admirable ability to dispassionately compartmentalize emotions. The distinct ability to step outside of oneself to be the observer. These, along with a law degree and a fair amount of legal knowledge, are all critical, essential qualities required of any judge. Judges can be detached and objective, and most do this well.

Judges, like police officers and first responders, can sit relatively stone-faced through the most gruesome, bloody, disarmingly violent narratives, while holding emotions intact as we sort through the legal ramifications of a given piece of evidence. We sift through horrific details and objects to assure that jurors don't receive evidence so emotionally jarring that it impairs their ability to be reasonable and objective. For example, will death by blunt trauma be clear to jurors merely by describing the bashed head lying in a pool of blood, or do jurors need to see a close up of the interior of the bloody, bashed head?

Judges make these types of decisions daily, seemingly without emotions. I say, seemingly because this writing project brought to the surface some scenes I sorted through in that same dispassionate manner. The ones that returned to mind most wrenchingly, involved women. These cases involved women who trusted someone, or women who "loved;" women looking for the "dream" life, or women wanting "that man." These women were the ones who suffered most.

Perfect Man

In one heart-wrenching case, a single mother of two daughters found, in her words, the "perfect man," only to learn that he molested both her twelve year old daughter and their infant daughter. We learned that he had routinely crawled into the bed of the oldest daughter, and fondled her, frightening her into secrecy. During a pediatric visit, the doctor discovered uncharacteristic bruises in her vaginal area. When confronted by the mother, her perfect man confessed to the molestation, then apologized profusely. The daughter's psychologist suggested that the healing process would be best served by allowing the daughter to confront him and tell him how much he hurt her. The courtroom was the safest place for this healing to occur.

During the most emotional sentencing hearing I ever experienced, we had to call repeated recesses so that the oldest daughter could collect herself to describe what this "perfect man" had done to her. Her mother literally held her in her arms as this young, violated girl told her horrific story. And, there was the girl's stoic grandfather who sat rigid, grave and tensed in the gallery, watching his daughter and his grand-daughter, while holding and consoling his shaking wife.

I had to call recess for the court reporter who could not see clearly enough to type through her tears, and for my own staff, who continuously dabbed at their eyes. The prosecutor could not raise her head to look at me, and even the defense counsel kept turning in his seat to stare at the back of the room, so his client would not see the tears glistening in his eyes. Then, there was me, the judge, seemingly detached and objective.

Mug Shot

In another case I was sentencing a woman whose mug shot was the scariest thing I'd ever seen. She had been arrested on drug possession and other charges. A photo was taken of her at the time of her arrest and it was the ugliest, scariest thing any of us had ever seen. Her eyes were bulged and protruding wildly. Her long, thick hair was standing on end as though she plugged herself into an electrical socket. Dirt clumps and green blades of grass clung to strands of her unkempt hair. Her skin was dirty and blotched with pits and scars. Her lips were chapped and dried, so she was not smiling.

The prosecutor, Lori Wada, had given me this photo of the female defendant during a sentencing hearing. Yet, the photo bore no resemblance to the stately, attractive and composed, well-coiffed Samoan woman who was standing before me. The defendant had made the most dramatic transformation of her life in the months between the mug shot and her court appearance that day. I showed her the picture several times just to be sure it was her. She smiled and assured me it was her, but she was never going back to that state again.

I had my staff make a copy of the mug shot, then I gave it to her and told her that should she ever have the urge to do drugs again just pull out the picture and remember where it had taken her. She thanked me. Months later, at a review hearing, she told me she had made several copies of the mug shot. She kept one in her wallet and pasted one on her bathroom mirror – a daily meditation reminder.

Tattooed Allegiance

She had his name engraved on her neck. When she tilted her head, or tied her hair up, you could see it clearly in bold script, a proclamation of her devotion.

Maile was "in love," but as it turns out, this wasn't really love; it was ice, batu, crystal methamphetamine. And this drug ripped her life apart. Maile was a young, single mother of Hawaiian extraction, with two beautiful children. Hers was a strong, traditional, *kama'aina* family that loved her and would do whatever they could to help this struggling mother. Maile's mother, her children's *Tutu*, was always available to watch the children, so Maile could go back to school, to work, or do whatever she needed to get her life on track. Maile had sisters, aunties, uncles, and a true *ohana*, or home. But, she "fell in love."

No one quite understood this mysterious man. Ben didn't show his face much. He didn't hang out with the family for weekend gatherings. But when Ben rang her cell phone, Maile was always ready to take off—daytime, nighttime, anytime. They laughed it off as the "booty call," which she always answered. He said he loved her, or so she told her family, but they didn't understand that kind of obsessive love. What kind of love would make you leave your children, continual fight with your mother and sisters, and avoid family events to be with him and him alone? The family realized this wasn't love, but something much more powerful and much more deadly. So, when Maile announced she was leaving the *ohana* to go live with Ben in his car, the line in the sand was drawn because the family could not help.

Maile and Ben moved into his car, a nondescript Toyota or Honda.

Maile left her children with their *Tutu* because *Tutu* was not going to allow Maile's babies to grow up into the madness of the ice world. Still hopeful, *Tutu* believed Maile would come to her senses, and certainly a mother's love would be stronger than the "love" Maile professed for Ben. Sadly, it wasn't. Late one night, Maile and Ben fell asleep in his car which he had parked in the car lot of a grocery store. In their dope-filled daze, they littered the dashboard with ice pipes, baggies and lighters. Honolulu police officers routinely patrolled this lot at night, so on this night an officer came upon the trespassing, sleeping lovers. The drugs and related paraphernalia were in "plain view."

Not surprisingly, Maile and Ben were taken to the local police station. One of the officers, Officer K knew her and her family. Since families don't usually share that kind of news even with close friends, this officer was surprised and hurt to see Maile in such a lost state. Officer K offered to help her, dump the guy, even to cut her a little slack, but Maile refused his help because she was in love, so she and her man would stick together, whatever happened. Maile assured Officer K that Ben loved her. After all, his name was tattooed in all its false glory, on her neck.

Both Maile and Ben were charged with multiple felonies, including felony possession of crystal meth. In Hawai`i at that time, possession of crystal meth carried a mandatory five year prison sentence. At the arraignment, the prosecutor sought to make a plea deal to insure at least one conviction. Criminal courts run on plea agreements; there's no way to do it otherwise, political posturing and hand-wringing to the contrary. When plea deals are being negotiated, they are discussed in the judges' chambers, not in open court. Criminal court judges set aside an entire afternoon each week for the sole purpose of determining whether cases go to trial or reach agreement.

A normal caseload would have ten to twelve cases poised to go to trial the following week. If an agreement is reached in chambers, then the parties come back in open court and state the agreement publicly, or "on the record." Once that is done, then the trial is called off, thus the witnesses won't be served with court summons, the police officers are told they don't have to come to court, and the chosen jurors are cancelled.

So, Maile was offered the deal first, but unfortunately, she refused it. She would not turn her back on her beloved because they would never turn on each other. There would be no deals. Once again she stated that they were in love. They would go down together. Her lawyer to say the very least, was not pleased.

Imagine what happened when the same deal was offered to him, her loyal lover. After a brief conversation with his attorney, Ben jumped at the deal, which included a requirement that he testify against Maile, if needed. Hey, he wasn't going to go down for five years for her, a fellow druggie. Who cared that his name was engraved on her neck? "Life is tough," he thought. He would have to make tough choices, so he chose to live without her.

When Ben agreed to the plea deal, he and his attorney returned to the courtroom to put the agreement "on the record." Unfortunately, Maile was still sitting in the courtroom when his agreement was being spelled out in open court. She was there because her case was set to proceed to trial. He could not, would not, look at her while Maile could not take her eyes off of him as the deal was meticulously spelled out. She was visibly stunned. Her eyes were pleading with him, but he did not see them because he resolutely looked anywhere but at Maile.

He would plead guilty to the felony possession of a "drug." In exchange, he would receive five years of probation with a brief period of incarceration, most of which had been completed, since he had not been bailed out between the time they were arrested and the time they came to court. He would also agree, if necessary, to testify at Maile's trial to the events of that fateful night. She was not prepared for this. Weren't they in love? Her so-called true love, her drug dealer had cost her everything—family, children, home, her future. Ice is many things, but love it is not.

After Maile's trial date was set, she would go to trial before a jury the following week. The state had all the evidence it needed. She sat there silently, clearly looking humiliated and abandoned. All eyes, some sympathetic, some accusatory, were on her—the prosecutor's, the sheriff's, the lawyers', and the onlookers' seated in the gallery. Maile sat alone, with only a useless name on her neck to keep her company.

When the trial began, it was an easy prosecution for the State. Maile decided to testify, perhaps in the hopes that the jury would understand that she was in love. I watched her on the witness stand as she was being cross-examined, hoping at every turn that she would not lift her hair in that unconscious manner that women often do because then everyone would see his name still tattooed on her neck. Ice will do that to you.

What was the end result? Well, the jury found Maile guilty of possession of crystal meth. A few weeks later, her sentencing hearing took place. Clearly, much had happened in the interim. What a different scene. Despite the fact that Maile was facing certain jail time, instead of suffering in isolation, she was surrounded by her *"ohana,"* her family. All of them were in the courtroom—her mother, her sisters, her children, even old friends. They were hugging Maile, crying for her, and assuring her of their unconditional love. They promised to care for her children, and to be there for her. After all, they had always been there for her, with or without a tattoo.

Even though incarceration for Maile's charges was mandatory, I felt certain that she would be released early into a treatment program by the Paroling Authority. I would like to believe that Maile will never be as alone and abandoned as she appeared on the fateful day when Ben took the plea deal. Fortunately for her, she still had her true family. And, if we look closely at ourselves, we might all realize that none of us are as alone as we imagine because there probably is somebody looking out for you too, just like there was eventually for Maile.

My Tattoo

There's another piece to this young woman's story that I have been reluctant to share until I went to a birthday celebration some years later for a friend. We chatted about my book plans and this particular defendant's story. As I shared the experience, attempting to maintain my detachment, this group of women immediately zeroed in on MY story. This situation bothered me, they all concluded because I didn't like sending her to jail, although I had to. They argued that during the trial, I knew that meth carried a mandatory jail term, like it or not, detached or not. I also knew that this poor child, and indeed Maile was a poor child, would go to jail while her no-good, turncoat, drug dealer boyfriend whose name was tattooed on her body –WOULD NOT! And, you know what? They were right.

Maile was as much a victim as she was now a convicted felon. And, yes, as detached and objective as I was in that judicial moment, this case bothered me like a tattoo knocking about in my head. This case hurt me. And yes, that tattoo silently angered me. The "lock 'em up and throw away the key" wave continues so long as residents believe that the only folk out there committing drug crimes are minority males. But now we see how young women, girls, teens, mothers, fathers, and "regular" folk suffer through their addictions. Suddenly, it is apparent that the whole community is affected whether using, dealing, or sincerely praying for a positive outcome for a friend or family member.

Our so-called war on drugs with its mandatory sentencing provisions so heavily touted as the ultimate cure for our crime-plagued streets had claimed another unnecessary victim. Were our streets now safe with Maile behind bars and Ben free to strike again? Did her mandatory sentence make us safer? I think not.

The tales of the lives that appear before judges sometimes read like fiction, but alas, they are all too real. But, it is not my intention to titillate readers by unveiling another's weaknesses by sharing these cases. What I do hope is for these situations and people to resonate with you even if you never appeared in court. Maybe you will stop, listen, learn, share, and change. Perhaps one day, you will be inspired to stop someone's suffering or your own.

Chapter 4

Real Cases, Real People

Lawyers are disciplined to view the world differently than most people. The myriad of issues that are brought to them tend to be viewed as "cases," rather than the human stories and tragedies that each represents. The discipline of "lawyering" stresses the ability to detach and be objective, which in turn enhances the lawyer's ability to sort through and define the legal question to be raised or resolved in the throes of the particular crisis appearing before him or her. For this reason, people generally call a lawyer when there is a problem.

Furthermore, our society places tremendous weight and responsibility on an admittedly small segment of the population—those trained and licensed to be lawyers—because lawyers are entrusted with the most intimate and important details of peoples' lives, their rights, liberty, property, happiness and finances. In law school, lawyers study the "case method" which entails analyzing and reviewing actual cases for the legal principles they represent, rather than the people and entities within them.

Therefore, when lawyers talk amongst themselves and evoke names like "Miranda," "Batson," or "Sullivan," the judgment and case details need not be repeated because every lawyer knows what each of these landmark cases stand for, even if they have no recollection of what individuals like Miranda or Batson did, or who Sullivan was. Those of us in the legal field study "the case of," not necessarily the people and entities *within* them. For example, we would discuss "the case about the Wong family," not what happened to individual members of this family. All of these objective elements are essential to the attorney's mindset. Otherwise, those of us in the legal field can lose the ability to focus on how best to represent the "client"—be she an individual, the state, a corporation, a group of people, or some other entity. Not surprisingly, an attorney's shield is always up.

While I was a judge, my shield was even more visible. Judges must be detached and objective too, since judges are often privy to the confidentialities and reports on *both* sides of the case, as well as that of independent professionals and experts who provide the details of their reports to judges, *in camera,* which means that both sides are assured that the reports are not shared with opposing counsel, or anyone else. Detaching from the individual is how judges need to think. So, my approach on the bench was one of pure objectivity, and of course, confidentiality.

A judge's neutrality, detachment and objectivity are relied on absolutely, by all sides, which is another reason why judges are required to disclose to all parties whether there are real or perceived conflicts that could possibly impede upon fair judgment. Thus, for me, in that process of assessing and maintaining that balance, I had to assure myself that I was not abandoning whatever "core" principles I brought to the bench.

So, when I spoke or made a ruling from the bench, I understood that my words carried weight and would affect a real person or entity. I understood that I was not merely ruling on a case; my ruling would inevitably make a difference in the life of a real person—the one standing right in front of me.

Diversity on the Bench

Let's face it – the lens with which we view life and yes, even the law, is going to vary based on our life experiences. Judges are still people too. This is a good thing and helps us understand why diversity, in and of itself, is as important as one's legal knowledge and experience. Judges who come from diverse backgrounds and experiences enliven their formal legal knowledge with the real life comprehension which in the long run, assures fairness in our justice system amidst our evolving communities.

Therefore, if a judge is a so-called minority who sees or experiences racism in her life, she most likely will exhibit more consideration for cases that might appear pointless to others, because she has shared these experiences. This doesn't mean the judge will rule in favor of the minority without reviewing the evidence, but she will be less likely to be dismissive of the case because it doesn't *seem* valid. For example, the daughter of a Japanese-American who watched as her parents were shuttled off to internment camps, or the native Hawaiian who saw ever-increasing numbers of Hawaiians shipped off to mainland prisons, might be more likely to be mindful of the cultural traditions and communal concerns underlining the facts of a given case. But I am not suggesting that these experiences alone can predict how a judge should, or even, may, rule.

However, what does occur on a diverse bench is that a judge's world view expands to consider the possibility that someone, indeed, the person standing in front of her, may have had a different life experience than her own.

Real Cases

I have ruled on intriguing cases that ranged from "run for the border" boys evading police cars on a small island, to the senseless violence of inebriated men brawling because someone received the "stink eye" when the bars closed on Hotel Street. Or, I recall the 76-year-old widow who kept the baseball bat by her bed and scared the stuff out of one hapless failure of a burglar.

And then there was the key witness in a gang murder case who had a unique stutter. Jake's testimony was filled with f-bombs, "f-f-fuckin" because that was his stutter pattern, so the more nervous Jake became, the more he stuttered and the more he cursed. The prosecutor, who was very experienced and rightly concerned that his key witness's coarse language would be a deal breaker for the case, made his *voir dire*, the questions during jury selection process, all about each juror's reaction to Jake's language.

In an act of pure brilliance, this prosecutor referred to Jake's curses as a "speech impediment," so he was able to receive assurances from the jurors that they would not hold Jake's inappropriate use of language against him. Defense counsel, equally experienced, I'm sure, had hoped for the opposite response. So, when this young eyewitness took the stand, it was clear that he was totally out of his element. He looked nervously from prosecutor, to me, to the defense, then to the jurors, and back again.

Now the questioning began. Regrettably, the f-word was in just about every sentence Jake spoke. And, to make matters more difficult, he stuttered when he cursed! I could see the jurors wincing each time a curse exploded in their ears. But as his testimony continued, their initial shock from his coarse language began to wear off. When Jake began to describe the harrowing events he witnessed, the f-bombs became less significant. By then the jurors were taking brisk notes.

Then it was time for cross-examination by the defense counsel. Unfortunately, Jake became even more nervous than before, so the f-bombs exploded more frequently. Fortunately for the prosecution, the jurors were, shall we say comfortable at this stage, and I noticed that they had settled into processing just the actual evidence, not Jake's colorful language. Sadly, Jake was friends with both the defendant, Joe, and the victim, Matt, of the drive-by shooting. Jake had been in the car with the defendant at the time of the shooting and saw Joe fire his gun into the passing car where Jake's other friend, Matt sat. Matt was fatally wounded. He was only 18 years old at the time of his death.

After the jury delivered their guilty verdict, I held my usual debriefing session with them. The trial had lasted about a week, so not surprisingly, the jurors had bonded. The deliberation room was aromatic from a large variety of pastries and home-baked goodies the jurors had shared during their deliberations. Despite the horrific events they had been made privy to, the jurors were in a rather festive mood.

They asked me various questions about the gang members, the witnesses, and even, about the fate of the defendant. Both attorneys also answered questions during our debriefing session. I thanked everyone for their services as they filed out the room when we finished. One of the jurors, a sprightly 82 year old, was walking towards the door, when suddenly, she stopped, turned and with a wry smile, wished all of us, a "good fucking evening!"

Stranger and Stranger

A few weeks later, I got a call from the defense attorney from this same case with an unusual request on behalf of his client, Joe, the young man who had fatally shot Matt and was about to be sentenced to life imprisonment. The attorney assured my secretary that it was not an "exparte," or one sided, communication about the case. So, what could it be then? Well, it turns out the defendant, Joe, wanted to get married before he was imprisoned, and he wanted me to perform the marriage ceremony! I declined of course, as he knew I would, so another judge performed the ceremony. As I stated earlier, you just never know what can turn up on the criminal bench.

In one particularly gruesome murder trial the victim was a middle-aged woman who had been brutally stabbed by a young man she had befriended. We learned that he tossed the knife into the Ala Wai Canal. Hawai`i is known the world over for our clean pristine beaches, clear waters and healthy air which is unmistakably true in general, but the Ala Wai Canal is neither clean, nor pristine, nor clear. In a word, it is generally regarded as grossly polluted. But the murder weapon was floating somewhere in there and the police needed to recover it as state's evidence.

The detective in charge of the investigation was a street savvy, cool, CSI type named Detective R who could be quite creative in his investigations. He needed someone to go into the Ala Wai Canal, but no police personnel were capable, nor was there anyone in the Fire Department. Detective R then contacted the sewage guys at Public Works, but even they said no because they did not have the equipment to go into the Ala Wai. This situation was becoming dire since one of the frightened witnesses was to testify that he was with the defendant when he tossed the knife into the murky waters.

It turned out that the only entity with personnel capable of scaling the floor of the canal was the United States Navy, more specifically, a Navy Seal named Will. Thus, on a bright sunny day (as most of our days in Hawai`i are) this young Navy Seal in full hazmat and diving gear, with cameras rolling, dove into the depths of the filthy Ala Wai waters while police photographers in the boat recorded his every move. It took a little while, but our Navy Seal found the weapon. Having accomplished *his* mission, Will was quite pleased when he emerged from the waters, whipped off his headgear and smiled broadly, as he hoisted the knife overhead in triumph! Mind you, the cameras were rolling, so this heroic retrieval would be introduced as evidence amid the grisly details of the murder trial.

At trial, the jurors first heard the harrowing testimony, and then they viewed the cheerful video of the blond, handsome, smiling Navy Seal emerging victorious from the depths of the Ala Wai with the recovered knife poised over his head, flashing a toothy smile. Priceless, utterly priceless.

Real Judgments

Clearly, the sheer authority with which a judge speaks carries weight well beyond the case. For this reason I was always mindful that when I sentenced a young person to significant prison time, my words at that moment would probably ring in that person's ears long after they left the courtroom. Thus, it was always important for me to assure that young person that he or she still held the key to their future. Consequently, their sentence and their incarceration were not the end of the world, but the consequence for their actions. The power to change their lives was still in their hands. My words probably did not remove their immediate fears or anxiety, so you might ask, "Why say them at all?"

The answer is that my words, like the ruling I make on cases, conveyed power and authority for defendants in my courtroom. If I continually berated these youth about their terrible crimes, now public record, or if I excoriated them as low-lives, unfit to walk the streets of society, most likely they would believe me and become repeat offenders. So instead, I remind defendants of their opportunity to choose a new path, to change. I think these words matters.

Words Matter, People Matter

Words. Words spoken from the bench matter. For instance, I've run into previously incarcerated folks throughout the community since I've been off the bench. Of course, these were the brave ones with enough confidence to walk up and greet me. Once in a line at Safeway, a guy called out "Hi Judge Simms!" I smiled and said "Hi" guardedly, unsure how I knew him. Because he was so ebullient, I assumed he had been a juror during one of my cases, so we struck up a light conversation. Finally, I said, "I'm sorry I don't remember your name." At that moment, he cheerfully told me I had sent him to jail! But no matter; he was doing just fine now. "I'm glad to hear it," I said before walking away, and I truly meant it.

Another time, a smiling, elegantly attired African American woman greeted me on the street. I returned the greeting even though I didn't recognize her. Black people in Hawai`i are so rarely seen that we often just speak or acknowledge each other on the streets even if we don't know each other. She paused to make some comment about my bench time and her court visit, but I could not remember who she was until she told me her name and her son's name Terell. I immediately remembered Terell and some of what I had said to him during his sentencing. He and another young man had committed a string of armed robberies for drug money a few years back.

I had given Terell a long sentence, 20 years to be exact, and my "not the end of the world" speech, specifically noted that his crime was not at all reflective of the sentencing report which detailed a picture of his caring family background. And now this young man's mother was greeting me on the street, reminding me of those words I spoke at that pivotal moment in her son's life. Terrell had been paroled and was doing well, finally.

My "cases" became real people. Even in the midst of the objectivity, detachment, and confidentiality that court cases demanded, I understood always that the decision I made, especially in criminal matters, affected a life, a real life, a real family, or sometimes even an entire community.

Chapter 5

Life After the Bench

As we know with all things and all people, change is inevitable; therefore, when the Judicial Selection Commission (JSC) announced that I would not be reappointed as Circuit Court Judge for the State of Hawai`i, I knew a shift in my life was occurring. Almost immediately, calls came in from all over—the local media, family and friends, here on the island and on the mainland. I received my share of happy crank callers too!

During interviews for the newspapers and television reporters, I spoke frankly, but I began to notice that I did not feel as lost as I thought I might. The media would ask, "How do you feel being the first African American woman to be appointed by former Governor John Waihe'e, who was not reappointed?"

My common response was "Not too good." But, as the barrage of coverage and media interest continued, my response shifted. "Life goes on," I told a reporter when he asked me about my current reaction. These words sprung up from a place deep inside me which I did not fully understand.

Interestingly enough, during 2003 several female judges either "retired" or "withdrew" their request for reappointment as their terms came to an end. I learned later through media reports that some of these "retirements" and "withdrawals" were not necessarily the individual choices of the judges, but rather because the JSC had requested that they retire or withdraw. I too was offered the option of withdrawing my request for reappointment, but, I chose not to.

For me, withdrawing was worse than standing my ground and relying on my service record. I was certain that my 13 years on the bench warranted reappointment. Plus, there was no way I could have explained to my family, who always supported me, why I would withdraw from seeking reappointment. So, Sandra Simms had to stand, not rigidly or doggedly in the midst of this unraveling chaos, but rather, stand in peace, committed to the oath I had pledged to serve the people of Hawai`i in the capacity of Circuit Court Judge. And, that was all.

The final decision of the JSC hurt, of course, but I had done the best job I could. Looking back, I could see nothing I would have decided differently. Nevertheless, I didn't enjoy being the butt of politically correct tirades for the sake of a rabid media, but judicial skin has to be tougher than that.

I was supposed to be angry by the JSC's decision not to retain my position, but I was not. Nor did I feel a sense of victimization or discrimination on any level. As I mentioned, life-altering events were swirling around me. My husband was being treated for prostate cancer, my son was dealing with a nest of legal problems, and my father had just died. This was a trying period for me, but my life had to "go on," if for no other reason than I had to get to a better place within me. There was no time for a pity party.

Being off the bench meant that I had time to care for and fully address these serious personal and legal issues in my family that needed my attention. Had I still been on the bench during this difficult period in my life, subject to the intense media scrutiny all criminal and felony judges experience, my family might not have emerged sound, healed, unified and empowered. Perhaps then, the JSC's decision was a blessing in disguise.

That same weekend of the JSC announcement, I was scheduled to attend my daughter's final Big Ten Championship meet held at Purdue University, so even then, there was little time to dwell on my situation. Vera was captain of the University of Michigan's women's track team and we were in the midst of discussing her future plans for graduate study and the possibility of her participating in the 2004 Olympic Trials. My life clearly was full of high peaks and low valleys.

In the past, whenever judges currently serving on the bench met up with recently retired judges, we always noted with joking envy that the retired judges looked younger, rested and more relaxed than the rest of us. Well, now I know there is a lot of truth in that because the calm demeanor of most judges belies the multiple duties and responsibilities we hold and perform on a daily basis. In fact, there is an unspoken, invisible and heavy weight on the shoulders of judges. So, despite my bruised ego, leaving the bench meant I could now smile a little easier, not worry so much, not carry so many secrets, and not bite my tongue so hard. Once more, I found time to use my voice for the people and things I cared most about.

Time to Grow

The following Tuesday, I went to my regular Soroptimist meeting at the Pacific Club. The Soroptimists' goal is to improve the lives of women and girls through their national and international programs. I was pleasantly surprised by the warm and positive response of club members to my retirement. Some women embraced me and some expressed relief that I was out of the "hot seat." One charter member with a quick and keen sense of humor, Anne Sutton, gleefully noted that I now had "three more lifetimes!" I was humbled by these good friends who steadfastly supported me in everything I did on the bench, and who joyfully rallied around me when I retired. It was time for me to go. And, time for me to grow.

As a result of my retirement I now had more time to participate in groups and causes that were important to me. I was already active with the Links Incorporated, a national service organization for professional women of color, and was president of our Hawai`i chapter. And suddenly, I was able to spend the summer of 2004 travelling and attending several annual conferences on the mainland for national organizations. In the space of a few weeks, the former presiding judge Sandra Simms was in Alberta, Canada for the Soroptimist Convention where women from around the world were making a difference in the lives of disadvantaged women through their philanthropic programs and contributions.

I chose to become more active, learning more and being more closely involved in our organization's Women's Opportunity Awards and the Fellowship Awards. At times, I found myself working alongside some of the same women I'd seen in court, only now these women had found a more positive outlet for their lives besides crime, drugs, alcohol, abuse or neglect. Here, their stories were of triumph and success, not failure and despair.

Through my work with the Soroptimists, we met a young woman named Kathryn Xian who was creating a weeklong conference on Oahu called "GirlFest." When we met Kathryn in 2004, human trafficking was not as widely discussed or understood as it is currently. Consequently, we were so inspired by her knowledge of the trafficking of young women and her passion for helping others, that along with my fellow Soroptimist Club members we embraced her work which we shared with our regional and international clubs.

That same year, I went to Charlotte, North Carolina for the National Bar Association (NBA) meeting, where I met trailblazing legendary lawyers and judges who welcomed and embraced me. The National Bar Association is the largest organization of African American lawyers and judges in the United States. The NBA (not to be confused with America's well-known basketball organization), was formed during 1925 when nearly all professional organizations barred Black professionals from joining. The American Bar Association did not open its membership to Black attorneys and judges until the 1940s, and similar bans existed for African American doctors and dentists who likewise created the National Medical Association and the National Dental Association.

I soon became involved with the NBA's International Affiliate programs to unite lawyers and judges from around the world. And, this organization involves itself in philanthropic work as well. For instance, while attending the NBA International Meeting in Ethiopia, I visited a center called "Desta Mender" outside Addis Ababa. There, I learned the horrors that young women in that country endured with "obstetric fistula," a hole in the birth canal which prevents a young female from holding her urine or feces.

Dr. Elizabeth Hamlin, an Australian national, founded Hamlin Hospital and Desta Mender, whose medical staff and volunteers perform corrective surgery for the women and girls free of charge. This issue moved me so much that when I returned to Hawai`i, I shared my concerns with fellow Links and Soroptimist members. Both organizations now have programs to help girls and women suffering from obstetric fistula in Africa. Truly, I was growing.

On Hawaiian Time

After my retirement, one of my close friends, the illustrious Dr.

Dorothy Goldsborough, Professor Emeritus, suggested I teach courses at a local university since I had given guest lectures in several of her courses over the years. I had never thought of myself as a teacher, let alone an academic, so this was a novel idea. The majority of my work experience was in criminal courts where esoteric legalistic machinations had little bearing, so, this idea of teaching did not appeal to me until I relented and actually taught an undergraduate course in Criminal Justice at Chaminade University of Honolulu. I loved it! I was a teacher!

But I was in for some illuminating and mildly surprising revelations. So few of my students knew much about our constitutional system and the history of its creation that I began to give each of them their own personal, pocket editions of the *United States Constitution!* They expressed amazement at times, at what it actually says as opposed to the media and partisan's grandstanding interpretations of its precepts. In fact, during my Introduction to Law class, my students were darn near stunned to read that the First Amendment did not create a nation based on Christ, yet so much had been extracted from it by partisans on all sides.

Clearly, the retired lifestyle I began to lead was replete with familial commitments, community activism, travel, academia, new and renewed friendships, and of course, the arts. My interest in art had been piqued years earlier by a deputy corporation counsel and colleague, the late Karl Ichida, who was an avid art collector. He introduced several of us to a fascinating and colorful world outside the law.

Karl whetted an appetite I was developing through my membership with the Links Incorporated. Links members had begun volunteering in several programs at the Honolulu Museum of Art, then called, the Honolulu Academy of Arts. Because of our participation, I met Karen Thompson, then Education Director for the Academy. I recall that one day I promised her I would be a docent when I retired.

Finally, that time had come, but I didn't realize that to become a docent at the Academy required two years of intense study and training for, as my children described it, a job that "does not pay." I signed up nonetheless, and my experience was glorious. I immersed myself in art collections, art history, indigenous and ancient cultures. I was fascinated with this new world of sensory delight. I had never had enough time for anything other than the study of law, even though I loved visiting museums and galleries while travelling. Consequently, after my docent training, my appreciation for the arts grew by leaps and bounds.

At this moment, I get quite a kick out of being the judge who became a docent because I learn something new every day and get to share a new passion with museum visitors, students, children and sometimes, the most unlikely of audiences. For example, during a recent "Tea and Tour" event at the Museum, I presented the topic "Crime and Art." This drew a maximum crowd of 20 for both days and the range of participants included an 80 year old woman who loved crime shows, to a visiting judge from the mainland, and an entire Pearl City family who were just curious. Not surprisingly, we had a ball!

My appreciation and love of the arts extended beyond Hawai`i. I met several renowned Black artists at Links' conferences in Beverly Hills, California, Boston, Massachusetts and Atlanta, Georgia. Once, I even shared a lunch table with the late Jacob Lawrence, internationally famous for his startling series of paintings that depict "The Great Migration" of African Americans from the South to Northern Cities after the failure of sharecropping. And, my involvement with The Links, and local black artists like John Nichols and Tabia Griffith, renewed my interest in black arts and black artists.

Life After the Bench

I've become a more conscious spiritual seeker, too. When anyone moves to Hawai`i from the mainland or anywhere else for that matter, Hawai`i's sheer beauty gives you faith in a higher power like nothing else. And, when you pair this with the energy of the people you meet, the "aloha spirit" still exists as your faith changes, or grows. God can no longer be limited to a Sunday morning exercise, or a public church service, because here, the spirit is everywhere. I just know there is a higher power which created this and created me, no matter what the odds.

I've come to know that my very public rejection of a judicial reappointment was also a very public lesson in how both to go and to grow. The lessons I learned in my early years from my parents, their parents, and our ancestors, have prepared me to handle just about anything the world could throw at me: opportunity, success, challenge, fear, acceptance, rejection, and yes, love. Armed with faith born of the lives and challenges of my ancestors, I could and I would grow, just in time.

My parents, Gerald and Vera Nuckolls
September 28, 1946

Sandra and Dad, 1952

Sandra and Raymond, 1952
Who knew she would grow up to be a judge?

Sandra's 5th Birthday Party
Backyard of 57th Wabash
July 26, 1953

Sandra's 5th Birthday Party
Backyard of 57th Wabash
July 26, 1953

Ribbons and party dresses

Sandra and Raymond dressed for church. 1957

Sandra, Raymond and David - chore time, 1957

Sandra at age 15.
Getting ready to be the life of the party with a
new "record player."

Judicial College in Reno, Nevada
1992

Swearing in, 1991

Judge Simms with wife of Senator Charles
Campbell, Naomi Campbell and Judge Eden Hifo.
1991

State of Hawai`i Judges, 1993

Judge Simms with Mayor Frank Fasi and Dr. Donnis Thompson,
the first Women's Athletic Director at the University of Hawai`i.

Newly appointed Circuit Judge Simms.
1994

Judge Simms on the bench.
1994

Hank and Sandra Simms

OFFICE OF THE MAYOR⬧
CITY AND COUNTY OF HONOLULU⬧

PROCLAMATION

WHEREAS, Sandra A. Simms has added an appointment as District Court Judge of the State of Hawaii to the milestones in her careers; and

WHEREAS, she is a native of Chicago where she was graduated from the University of Illinois and DePaul University College of Law; and

WHEREAS, upon receiving her degrees, she moved to Honolulu with her husband and took a position as a law clerk in the Hawaii Intermediate Court of Appeals; and

WHEREAS, Sandra was appointed as Deputy Corporation Counsel with the City and County of Honolulu, first in the Family Support Division and then in the Counselling and Drafting Division where she made substantial contributions to our local government policies and operations for nearly 10 years; and

WHEREAS, after a short period with the State Attorney General's Office of Information Practices, she was sworn in as District Court Judge earlier this month; and

WHEREAS, she is being honored by her husband, Hank, their children, Sharon, Vera, and Richard, friends, and colleagues at a special dinner on November 30, 1991,

NOW, THEREFORE, I, FRANK F. FASI, Mayor of the City and County of Honolulu, do hereby proclaim November 30, 1991, as

SANDRA A. SIMMS DAY

in the City and County of Honolulu and extend heartfelt congratulations on her well-deserved new position.

IN WITNESS WHEREOF, I have hereunto set my hand and caused the Seal of the City and County of Honolulu to be affixed.

Done this 29th day of November, 1991, in Honolulu, Hawaii.

FRANK F. FASI, Mayor
City and County of Honolulu

Judge Simms' Proclamation

HAWAII JOINT POLICE ASSOCIATION

Certificate of Distinguished Service

Is awarded to

**The Honorable
Judge Sandra Simms
Judge of the First Circuit Court, Hawaii**

In recognition of her outstanding performance on the bench the
FAA as a role model for men and women in government. Judge
Simms dedication, hard work and technical knowledge have
earned for her the admiration and respect of us all.

May 3, 2002
President

Ellie Kaanaana
Ellie Kaanaana,

Judge Simms' Joint Police Award

Letter to Judge Simms

Honorable Judge Simms,
Thank you for letting us meet you and welcoming us in your courtroom. I learned how hard it is to be a judge but maybe I'll be one someday.

YOUR FRIEND,
LEHUA KAMAKAWIWOOLE

Letter to Judge Simms

2301 Pauoa Road
Honolulu, Hi 96813
February 11, 1997

Dear Judge Simms,

Thank you for coming to our school. I really learned a lot and wish I could learn more. I especially liked when you talked about the three branches: the Executive, Legislative, and Judicial branch. My favorite branch is probably the Judicial branch. I like it because they make sure that the law gets carried out. I also enjoyed when you taught us how they pick the jury. I didn't know that they ask each person Individually.

I think I would love to be a judge. I don't know what kind, probably a family judge. At first I thought being a was kind of lame, but after you told us more about what judges do, it sounds fun.

I hope you get to come back to our school someday and teach other kids about what a judge is exactly. I know that I would love to hear more, and they would too.

Sincerely,

Jamie Abe

Letter to Judge Simms

2301 Pauoa Road
Honolulu, Hawaii 96813
February 5, 1997

Dear Judge Simms,

    I am a sixth grader at Pauoa School who saw your presentation. I enjoyed the talk you gave about being a judge. That is why I wrote this letter.
    The parts I liked about the presentation most were when you talked about how many cases that you had and what you did.I learned that there are four ways of rating crimes and how long you have to stay in jail for them. I also enjoyed the talk about why you became a judge.
    I liked this presntation most of all because it gave me something to think about. I might someday want to become a judge too.

Sincerely,

Michael Ching

Letter to Judge Simms

2301 Pauoa Rd.
Honolul , HI 96813
February 12,1997

Dear Judge Simms ,
My name is Tania Liufau . I am a 6th grader at Pauoa School . I have 2 brothers and no sister . I'm 11 years old.

I would like to thank you for coming to our school and talking to us about being a judge . I have learned alot from you , like the 3 brancjes are the Judicary Branch , Executive Branch and the Legislative Branch. Iknow now that there is no death penalty in Hawai'i but you could only sentence them for life.

I hope you come here to our school again . I think the students next year would also enjoy having you .

Sincerely Yours,

Tania Liufau

Judge Sandra Simms teaching class.

NOVEMBER 2, 2007

TINA YUEN PBN

Retired Circuit Court Judge Sandra Simms teaches a class on criminal justice at Windward Community College. The Windward students will be able to pursue four-year degrees from Chaminade University, where Simms also teaches.

Windward students find new roads to 4-year college degrees

EDUCATION

BY NANEA KALANI
PACIFIC BUSINESS NEWS

Finding it inconvenient to travel outside her Windward Oahu community, Karlotta Carvalho, like most Windward Community College students, was deterred from attending a university in central Oahu.

"The traffic time spent on the road and finding parking isn't worth it," Carvalho said of the commute that can take up to an hour each way.

But through a new program in place at Windward, Carvalho is taking bachelor-level courses toward a criminal justice degree without having to travel into Honolulu.

The offering is part of the college's initiative to create partnerships with four-year universities, including ones outside the University of Hawaii system, to offer advanced-degree programs at Windward.

Data shows that students generally don't go on from a community college to pursue a four-year education unless the school is in their area, according to Windward Chancellor Angela Meixell.

She said that is especially true of Windward students, who tend to be older and have children, jobs and other responsibilities.

Windward, which is accredited to offer only certificates and two-year degrees, created an office of university partners last spring to focus on the four-year initiative. It has an arrangement with Chaminade University to offer introductory courses in criminal justice and forensic science. Chaminade faculty members teach the courses at Windward.

Carvalho

"I think this is a great partnership because the program acts as a feeder from our school into Chaminade," said Carvalho, who is working on a psychosocial associate degree. "By the time I finish my associate degree, I already will have my feet wet with this bachelor program."

Carvalho, 44, said she took a professor's advice to pair her current degree with Chaminade's criminal justice program.

With 19 students enrolled in the two Chaminade courses, four additional criminal justice courses have been set up for the upcoming spring semester, said Connie Turner, coordinator for the Office of University Partners.

Tuition goes to both schools. For criminal justice classes, students pay Chaminade $131 per credit hour. For general education courses taken at Windward, students pay $63 per credit to the community college.

The earned degree is from the partner school, not from Windward.

For the criminal justice program, students also can take Chaminade classes offered both online and at the Kaneohe Marine Corps Base, in addition to the courses offered on the Windward campus.

Turner said Windward also is completing plans to begin offering an interior design degree from Chaminade next spring. In addition, it is working toward offering an elementary education degree from UH-West Oahu some time next year, as well as a veterinary technician program in the future.

The Chaminade programs were chosen because those degrees are not available in the University of Hawaii system.

Turner said Windward hopes to eventually offer entire degree programs on the campus as student interest increases.

nkalani@bizjournals.com | 955-8001

New judges

■ Waihee picks two women . . .

We're pleased that Gov. John Waihee has selected two respected District Court judges — Victoria Marks and Sandra Simms — for promotion to the Circuit Court bench. We expect they will readily win Senate confirmation.

Simms

Marks

Judge Marks is the wife of Attorney General Robert Marks. Her nomination comes just a year after Waihee's ill-fated nomination to the Supreme Court of Sharon Himeno, wife of former Attorney General Warren Price, touched off a bitter confirmation battle.

Amid "insider" charges against Waihee, the state Senate took the unusual step of refusing to confirm Himeno.

But Himeno had no judicial experience, although she is a successful attorney. Judge Marks, in contrast, has served on the Family Court since 1988

and seen temporary duty at Circuit Court.

Judge Simms also has experience at District Court and at the state Attorney General's Office and Honolulu Corporation Counsel.

These two appointments enhance Waihee's record for putting qualified women in important positions. He now has named 11 women to the bench. In a further stroke for diversity, Judge Simms is an African American.

We're glad to see Waihee continue to release all the names recommended to him by the Judicial Selection Commission. But we still think that Waihee — and whoever succeeds him — should do even more to dispel the public's sense of powerlessness by releasing the names when he gets them, before the choice is made.

■ . . . but Salling isn't qualified

In January 1993, Herman Lum, then chief justice of the state Supreme Court, appointed Michael Salling, then a Kauai attorney, to serve as a District Court judge on Oahu.

But Salling was saddled with some unwelcome baggage — complaints filed by former clients alleging unethical conduct and neglect.

So his oath of office was put on hold, pending disposition of those complaints.

Now the Supreme Court has acted on the complaints and suspended Salling from the practice of law for six months.

Salling is the husband of a state senator, Lehua Fernandes Salling. As in the case of Judge Victoria Marks, discussed above, the question isn't who these nominees are married to, but whether they are individually qualified to serve.

Marks is. Salling is not.

IN HAWAII

Appointees sailing through

Judicial nominees may be Waihee's last

By Peter Rosegg
Advertiser Capitol Bureau Chief

Not a discouraging word was heard yesterday as the latest, and probably last, of Gov. John Waihee's judicial appointments breezed through Senate confirmation hearings.

The names of Family Court Judge Victoria Marks and District Court Judge Sandra Simms, both appointed to circuit court judgeships, will go to the full Senate for approval with the blessing of the screening committee, said Sen. Ann Kobayashi, who chairs the Executive Appointments Committee.

Not even mentioned at the hearings was the fact that Victoria Marks is the wife of Waihee's attorney general, Robert Marks. AG Marks submitted testimony on behalf of Simms, but none for his wife.

Kobayashi said a Waihee

Marks   Simms

nomination on hold in the face of strong opposition is that of Libert Landgraf, former Department of Land and Natural Resources deputy director, to the board that oversees that department.

Environmental groups and individuals testified against Landgraf, saying he had been a poor administrator and was not concerned enough about protecting natural resources. The committee has given Landgraf

three pages of questions to answer before a decision on his nomination can be made.

Another appointment that may be held up is Phyllis Fox, of the Historic Hawaii Foundation, to the State Foundation on Culture and the Arts. Fox has only recently moved to the Big Island and artists and others there do not feel she adequately represents them.

Kobayashi also said her committee would likely be sending the name of professional lobbyist George "Red" Morris to the Senate for approval of his nomination to the Hawaii Community Development Authority.

There was considerable testimony against Morris because of his high-profile lobbying on behalf of a long list of business clients. But none of the testimony clearly indicated Morris would not do a good job, Kobayashi said.

Waihee names two to court vacancies

Star-Bulletin staff

Two women have been appointed by Gov. John Waihee to be First Circuit Court judges.

District Family Judge Victoria S. Marks was appointed to the Third Division and District Judge Sandra A. Simms to the 12th Division.

Marks replaces Judge Leland Spencer who retired. Marks has been a Family Court judge since 1988. She graduated from Miami University of Ohio and the University of Cincinnati College of Law.

Simms, a District judge since 1991, replaces Judge Simeon R. Acoba Jr. who was appointed to the Intermediate Court of Appeals. The nominees must be confirmed by the Legislature.

Other candidates, submitted to Waihee by the Judicial Selection Commission, were Elwin P. Ahu, Gary B.K.T. Lee, Florence Nakakuni, Marcia J. Waldorf and James H. Dannenberg.

Female judicial nominees treated same as male counterparts

In Rob Perez's June 1 article on alleged bias against women seeking or holding judgeships, a comparison was made between judicial nominees Michael Broderick and Simone Polak, which alluded that they were equal in not having experience in family court, yet were treated disparately by the bar 'association. This allusion is faulty because they are not equal.

Their educational backgrounds are leagues apart. Borderick graduated with honors from the University of Southern California's School of Law, which is ranked as the 18th-best law school in the nation by US News and World Report. Polak, on the other hand, graduated from the University of the Pa-

cific Law School, which is ranked as a third-tier law school by US News. Law schools on the lowly third tier are not ranked in numerical order.

Contrary to what was stated in the news article, Broderick has experience with the Family Court, when he served as the head administrator of the court system. In that capacity, Broderick had first-hand knowledge of the types of cases being presented to the Family Court, the duration of those cases, the outcomes of those cases, the rate of reversals on appeal and the reasons for reversal on appeal.

Regarding the statement that female judges are demure and unassertive and therefore criticized as inferior, I know of no

more of an assertive, vocal and verbally opinionated judge than Riki Amano. Those who have appeared before her would never call her demure. I am sure that the Judicial Selection Commission and the bar association did not rank her based on reticence.

Too little is mentioned of the competent female judges who were nominated and retained by the JSC. For example, the article makes no mention of highly competent female judges like Linda Luke, Marie Milks and Leslie Hayashi, all of whom graduated from Georgetown Law, which is ranked the 13th-best law school, or Colleen Hirai and Allene Richardson Suemori, both of whom graduated from the University of Cali-

fornia's Hastings College of Law, or of Frances Wong, who graduated from USC Law.

Finally, I am of the opinion that women who are seeking judicial appointments are treated equally by both the bar association and the JSC. Indeed, I am confident that both bodies are sensitive to the fact that historically women have been underrepresented on the bench. However, while being sensitive to this fact, they cannot shirk their responsibility to ensure that only competent people, irrespective of gender, are appointed to judgeships.

Charles K.Y. Khim,
Attorney at law
Honolulu
Georgetown Law Class of 1980,

Advertiser photo by Gregory Yamamoto

Hawaii's newest district judge

Sandra A. Simms was sworn in yesterday as a district judge in Hawaii by Chief Justice Herman Lum. Simms, 43, is a graduate of DePaul University College of Law.

NEWSMAKER

Making the law work for all

At times, Sandra Simms' life has sounded like a Nike commercial. When she wanted something done, she would just do it.

"We were taught to set goals, work toward it and do it," she says about her childhood, growing up in Chicago. "Once I decided to go into law, it was do it."

So she did it. After graduating from law school, she moved with her husband to Hawaii and began her law career, working first as a law clerk for Yoshimi Hayashi, then chief judge of the Hawaii Intermediate Court of Appeals.

Simms then spent nearly 10 years as a city deputy corporation counsel before moving to the state attorney general's office of information practices. This month she became a district court judge.

"I got into law, in my generation, with the sincere desire to contribute to society," Simms says, "to see our society change to be the kind of environment that we can all feel was fair."

Like many children of the civil rights movement, Simms recognized her responsibility to achieve what her parents were denied.

"I was the first in my family to attend college. That was just expected, to do that."

The oldest of three children and the only daughter, Simms credits her parents and the black community church for providing a nurturing and supportive environment.

Although life for her children is somewhat different growing up in the multicultural society here, Simms continues to instill the self-esteem and confidence in her children that she received from her parents.

"Minority children simply have to be. There's no choice," she says. "The history of our country teaches us that certain things, as a society, we haven't overcome totally.

"As a parent, as a minority parent, I have to prepare my children to deal with those things . . . And not let those factors deter them from accomplishment, achievement, learning or just living."

Benjamin Seto, Star-Bulletin

Name: Sandra A. Simms
Age: 43
Position: District Court judge
Education: U. of Illinois; DePaul University College of Law
Interests: Reading, tennis, community work, time with 3 kids

MidWeek August 29, 2001 59

A Down-to-earth, Friendly Judge

FROM PAGE 58

and the encyclopedia yearbook came out the next year, we couldn't understand why his death wasn't included.

"We did everything at the church. It wasn't just a religious institution. The church provided the leadership for the civil rights movement. It did community development. It provided tutoring programs for the schools, and it provided scholarship programs for young Afro-American kids who needed help with college."

Simms remembers a Sunday in the mid-1960s when the Rev. Martin Luther King visited the Apostolic Church of God: "The crowd was huge. I couldn't see King, but I could follow his progress through the congregation as people went silent in waves as he approached."

Sandra Simms was born Sandra Nuckolls in 1948 in the South Shore area of Chicago. She was the oldest of three children of Gerald and Vera Clemons Nuckolls. Her father, a tailor by training, had moved from Bloomington, Ill., to Chicago where he took a job with a men's clothing-store chain.

Her mother, besides rearing three children, always held a full-time job: as a secretary and timekeeper for a plating company, as a secretary for the city of Chicago, and as a financial aid counselor at Kennedy-King College.

"Bloomington was a college town, but there was an unspoken rule that blacks couldn't go past high school. So it was a given in my family that we were going to college," Simms remembers.

Provided you could make it that far. Simms admits to having been "spoiled as a child and a little on the edge. I never did anything crazy-crazy. I was brought up middle class among conservative church people."

Her father remembers her as "an avid reader at a very young age" and as "very intense. She had her own mind," says Gerald Nuckolls. "Her mother and I had to learn to cope with her."

The Nuckolls had help with their children, for they were surrounded by relatives. Her grandfather Clemons was one of 16 children, and he brought his brothers, his sisters and his neighbors north to Chicago and an eight-unit apartment building he had purchased. "It was wall-to-wall relatives," says Simms.

Sandra Nuckolls was a good student but, in her words, "verbal." In the seventh grade her principal translated "verbal" into "incorrigible" and sent her to a school for incorrigibles.

"Sandra was always very smart and very busy," her father remembers. "So she'd finish her schoolwork before the others, than she'd talk and bother them.'

"Her teacher told us that she'd never amount to anything. My wife was in tears."

The principal couldn't understand why such a bright young girl had been sent to her school, so Sandra spent the year tutoring the incorrigibles.

Sandra Nuckolls graduated from Hyde Park High School in 1966, then matriculated at the University of Illinois's new Chicago campus. She majored in sociology and political science, graduating in 1971.

To support her studies, Nuckolls became a flight attendant for United Air Lines. She also started law school at Chicago's DePaul University (where her classmate was Carole Mosley Brown, the first African-American woman to serve in the U.S. Senate).

"That was one of her mother's traits," Gerald Nuckolls remembers. "She always pushed Sandra to go ahead in life.

"Sandra was never content with just an answer. She had to ask another question: Why? When? Where? Who? She always wanted to question and debate. So we told her she'd better go into a field where her mouth could make money for her. Maybe a lawyer."

While working as a flight attendant, Sandra Nuckolls met and married fellow UAL employee Hank Simms. By the time she graduated from law school in 1978, Simms was pregnant with the couple's second child. She was also in transit, because United offered Hank the post of in-flight service director in Honolulu.

In 1980, Simms took a clerkship with Justice Yoshimi Hayashi at the Intermediate Court of Appeals. She stayed there for a year-and-a-half, then went to work at the office of Honolulu's Corporation Council. "I did everything there," Simms remembers, "drafting bills, counseling, family support."

Her boss at corp. counsel was Naomi Campbell, and Simms credits Campbell with doing much to form her: "Naomi had such a strong sense of compassion for people, and particularly for children and single mothers.

"She listened to every new client as if it was the first case she'd ever heard. She never grew jaded. She never lost her sense of compassion for people."

Campbell's sense of compassion echoed that of Judge Hayashi with whom Simms had clerked. Attorney Cora Avinante worked

with Simms at the corporation council office: "We were in the child support division, helping collect child support from deadbeat dads. Sandra was a good, consistent lawyer who was very astute about what's going on in the whole process of the legal system."

In 1991, Hawaii Supreme Court Chief Justice Herman Lum tapped Simms for a District judgeship. In 1994 an opening occurred for a 10-year term as a Circuit Court judge. Simms applied and got it.

From clerkship to corporation counsel to the judicial bench, Simms has also been involved in rearing three children — two girls and a boy. How did she balance it all?

"I'm not sure you do," she says. "You make some choices: some things you can do, and some things you can't.

"I chose government law rather than private practice because it allowed more time for family. But it was hectic. I always said that work at corp. counsel was a piece of cake. The hardest part of my day with three children was just getting out of the house in the morning."

Simms did far more than get out of the house in the morning. Besides her job, she played an active role in the Mililani Parent-Teachers Association. All three of her children attended public schools and graduated from Mililani High School. Simms also found time to serve on the

Mililani Neighborhood Board.

She's also been heavily involved with the Soroptimists, the oldest women's service club in the country. In Hawaii, the club has been supporting programs to help single parents return to the work force. Whatever remaining time she has, Simms gives to Links, a national Afro-American service club.

"Sentencing is the most important thing you do as a judge," says Sandra Simms. "And you have to balance public safety with a determination of whether the defendant can be a productive citizen.

"Sentencing is particularly troubling because so many of the people who come before me are so very young. Nationally, the notion is that we should crimi-

nalize acts that were once considered pranks. But condemning a young person as a piece of scrap is a very serious matter.

"Certainly some things warrant incarceration. I try to tell those whom I send to prison that it is not the end of the world. They must pay the consequences of their acts, then proceed on.

"I recently sentenced a 19-year-old man to 20 years in prison. I pointed out to him that when he gets out he will still be a young man. He can use his time in prison to become a better criminal or to make a new life. I urged him to do the latter."

Simms shrugs off criticism of her decisions, and rejects the notion that she would ever compromise her best judgment for another 10-year term as a judge. "I'd love to be loved," she says. "We all would. But popularity should never be the basis of judicial decision-making."

She has her own criticisms of the criminal justice system in which she operates. "We need more drug-treatment facilities for people," she says. "We need a realistic view of how devastating drugs are on families and society. We don't have nearly enough treatment facilities to deal with the size of the problem."

Despite the criticism she has received, despite the isolation of the job, Sandra Simms likes being a judge.

"If you like the law, and I always have, the bench is the best place to practice it," says Simms.

"But more important, a judge is in a position to have an impact on a person's life. At sentencing, the judge's words are the last that the defendant will hear. And those words can make a difference, particularly with young people, between becoming a productive citizen or being condemned to a life of crime."

Fortunately for those who come before her, Sandra Simms would prefer to see productive citizens engaged in a good world.

28 MidWeek August 29, 2001

COVER STORY

A Judge Who Can Take The Heat

Judge Sandra Simms says her job is a balancing act — between public safety and rehabilitation

By DAN BOYLAN

The hardest part about being a judge? "Judicial isolation," says 52-year-old Circuit Court Judge Sandra Simms.

"People treat you differently, even your friends. They're very careful how they communicate with you so that they don't unduly influence you. Then there's the security. We're surrounded by locked doors and metal detectors.

"There's camaraderie in a law office. People chat with one another. There's a lot of good fun. That's not the case for a judge."

For Sandra Nacholis Simms, judicial isolation must be particularly difficult. She's known as a friendly, open member of the bench.

"She's very down-to-earth, humble and friendly," says attorney Daphne Barbee-Wooten.

"She's very loving and very supportive. She's one of the nicest people I know," says fellow Circuit Court Judge Marie Milks — a sentiment echoed word-for-word by a member of the city prosecutor's office.

Simms smiles easily and speaks to co-workers in the hallways and on the elevator. One lunch hour a week she meets with a quilting group at a location which, for security reasons, she won't disclose. She's a gourmet cook who has been known to invite students far from home into hers for a holiday meal.

Yet in the opinion of some, Sandra Simms may be too nice. Her critics cite a series of decisions in 1998 and 1999 in which she left the jaws of prosecutors and many in the community hanging down near their breastbones.

Judge Sandra Simms sees a "good world" because she grew up in one

"People treat you differently, even friends. Then there's the security."

Simms allowed a Waianae man convicted of punching and breaking the jaw of a 17-year-old while on probation to remain out of jail for three-and-a-half months so he could bond with a newborn son.

She cut a 10-year term in half for a man convicted of driving under the influence for the third time in a year.

And Simms imposed a token 30-day jail sentence on a man who had violated his parole twice after being convicted of theft in connection with the savage beating and robbery of a tourist on the North Shore.

Editorialists, columnists, elected officials, and prosecutors came down hard on Simms. In the case of the man who robbed the tourist, City Prosecutor Peter Carlisle deemed Simms' decision "a clear display of excessive leniency."

About Simms' judicial record in general, Carlisle said in 1999: "From a prosecutorial perspective, there have been too many chances given to defendants at the risk and safety of the public and (that) gives the appearance of a toothless judicial system as far as this judge is concerned."

Honolulu Weekly cartoonist John Pritchett was not so diplomatic. He drew

Judge Simms confers with law clerk Michael Wong

Judge Simms smiling down from the bench on Adolf Hitler and Attila the Hun, says Pritchett's Simms: "You've violated parole again. You're born bad boys! But ... well ... OK, I'm going to give you another chance. Come see me again in six months."

Beside the bench Pritchett's large-nosed bailiff says to Adolf and Attila: "Don't forget your fruit basket on the way out."

"That was a terrible cartoon in the *Honolulu Weekly*," says attorney Barbee-Wooten. "You have to look at all of a judge's decisions to be fair, not just a few controversial ones. Judge Simms has come

"Popularity should never be the basis for judicial decision-making."

down with many harsh sentences as well.

"She's a compassionate person on the bench, a type sorely lacking in both the Hawaii judicial system and nationally. She listens to both sides in the case, and even after sending someone to prison she tries to see that he gets the programs he needs to be rehabilitated. She cares a lot, and that's refreshing."

Circuit Judge Marie Milks has known Simms and her work for 20 years, and she does not see her as a particularly lenient judge. "She's in the range of things, certainly not an extremist," says Milks. "She's thoughtful, sincere, committed, and she works hard. She's neither radical or off the wall. I'm sure that if you asked anyone in the probation department about Judge Simms' record, they would tell you she's not off the chart or too lenient — that she sits right in the middle of the judges when it comes to incarceration versus parole."

Milks stresses that care should be used in criticizing a judge. "I might very well have done the same thing in those cases that Judge Simms did," says Milks. "We don't have the pre-sentencing report and sentencing recommendation prepared by the probation officers. We don't have all the facts the judge has.

"Judge Simms sees a good world. She's a nurturing person who recognizes the redeeming qualities in people. If a judge can't see the positive aspects of people, can't recognize the redeemable qualities, I think it's time to get out of this line of work."

If Sandra Simms "sees a good world," it's because she was born and reared in one. As for so many African-Americans growing up in post-war America, a nurturing church constituted the center of her life.

Hers was the Apostolic Church of God in the Woodlawn section of Chicago's South Side, a church founded by her maternal grandfather, the Rev. Walter Mack Clemons (and where her 80-year-old father is currently the senior deacon).

"My grandfather was larger than life," she remembers. "We thought he was the coolest thing around. When he died in 1959

SEE PAGE 59

Judge rebukes gun toter's 'Rosa Parks' statement

By LINDA HOSEK
Star-Bulletin

A man convicted of carrying a loaded pistol into a Zippy's Restaurant got probation instead of a prison term, but didn't score any points with the judge when he compared himself to civil rights activist Rosa Parks.

Circuit Judge Sandra Simms yesterday sentenced Steven Stefanov to two five-year terms of probation, to run concurrently, for carrying a pistol without a license and keeping an unloaded rifle in his truck April 2 at the Waiau Zippy's.

But she also rebuffed his analogy, telling the gun-rights advocate who draped himself in the American flag during his trial, "You're no Rosa Parks."

Parks, an African American woman, refused to sit in the back of a public bus in Alabama on Dec. 1, 1955, leading to historic civil rights laws.

Deputy Prosecutor Dan Oyasato had asked for the maximum terms of 10 years for the pistol and five years for the unloaded rifle offenses.

"I didn't feel he was an appropriate candidate for probation because of his open defiance of the

system, authority, and the law," Oyasato said out of court.

During his opening statement, Stefanov said the U.S. Constitution guarantees his right to openly carry a gun. He said he didn't have a problem with rules or regulations, adding the state has a right to require gun registration and that he had registered his guns.

Oyasato said Stefanov carried into the restaurant a fully loaded .45 caliber semiautomatic pistol in a holster and had two additional seven-round clips with ammunition.

He said Stefanov had an unloaded semiautomatic rifle in a gun

case behind the front seat. In his truck and had a box with ammunition for several types of firearms.

As a probation condition, Simms said Stefanov cannot possess or own firearms.

Stefanov said he would comply, but Oyasato raised doubts: "He's going to defy the law again. He doesn't think he did anything wrong."

Oyasato said Stefanov would have access to firearms through his association with Hawaii Unorganized Militia.

State firearms laws prohibit individuals from carrying loaded or unloaded firearms in public.

WEDNESDAY • APRIL 23, 2003   E-mail: hawaii@HonoluluAdvertiser.com

Wai'anae teen gets 20 years

Prosecutor sought life for '01 beating death

By David Waite
ADVERTISER COURTS WRITER

A 17-year-old Wai'anae youth was sentenced in Wai'anae District Court yesterday to up to 20 years in prison for his part in the July 14, 2001, beating death of William Van Winkle.

Victor Faagau, who was 15 at the time of the incident, was one of five youths charged with punching and stomping Van Winkle to death after he rode a bicycle up to the group of young men at the park. Faagau was the last of the assailants to be sentenced.

Van Winkle's partially clad body was found on a park recreation court the following morning by a passing jogger.

At the end of a jury-waived trial that ended in December, Circuit Judge Sandra Simms found Faagau guilty of manslaughter instead of second-degree murder, saying that contradictory evidence kept her from concluding beyond a reasonable doubt that Faagau was guilty of the more serious charge.

Conviction on the murder charge would have required Simms to sentence Faagau to a mandatory life term with

the possibility of parole.

Because she found Faagau guilty of manslaughter instead of murder, Simms had four different sentencing options from which to choose yesterday. She could have sentenced Faagau to probation and up to a year in jail; to no more than eight years in prison as a youthful offender; to no more than 20 years; with the Hawai'i Paroling Authority to determine how much time he would have to serve before being eligible for parole; or to find that Faagau's level of dangerousness warranted an extended prison term of life

with the possibility of parole.
Faagau's lawyer, Myles Breiner, urged Simms to sentence Faagau as a youthful offender. But city Deputy Prosecutor Franklin Pacarro Jr. sought an extended term. He asked Simms to continue the sentencing hearing so that two of the three mental health experts who examined Faagau after he was found guilty could finish their reports on Faagau's dangerousness in hopes the reports might bolster the prosecution's request for an extended term.

Pacarro said Simms denied the request to continue the matter. According to Pacarro, Simms said the record in front of her provided enough information to

sentence Faagau to the 20-year term.

"She didn't allow us to put on the case for the extended sentencing," Pacarro said after the hearing. "The proper thing would have been to let the doctors opine about how dangerous Mr. Faagau is, or is not," Pacarro said.

"Obviously, she's not concerned for the community's safety or for that matter, about the rights of the defendant" since the two doctors who didn't file their reports may have found that Faagau was not dangerous, Pacarro said.

Simms declined to comment on the matter.

Even though Simms did not grant the eight-year term he sought for Faagau, Brein-

er said Pacarro's criticism was uncalled for.

"I think it's unprofessional and sets a bad precedent to the prosecution to attack a sitting judge when her ruling was supported both by the facts and the law," Breiner said.

When Simms found Faagau guilty of manslaughter instead of murder, it should have been clear to the prosecutor's office that the judge would not likely grant a request for an extended term of life with parole, which would have been the required sentence had Simms found Faagau guilty of murder, Breiner said.

Reach David Waite at dwaite@honoluluadvertiser.com or 525-8030.

A-18 ☐ Friday, January 10, 1997

Balbirona asks for 2nd chance

By LINDA HOSEK
Star-Bulletin

Valerie and Allen Balbirona hope to bail their son Rodney out of jail so he can show the judge he's changed before his Feb. 13 sentencing for stealing from a Chicago police officer, who was severely beaten in the April incident.

"The love of his family will keep him straight," Valerie Balbirona said out of court, adding that her 19-year-old son has learned from being in prison since his arrest that "he has to work for his money and not take it from others."

Circuit Judge Sandra Simms yesterday reduced bail for Rodney Balbirona from $20,000 to $5,000 to reflect his conviction for second-degree theft.

> **Rodney Balbirona said that he didn't want to return to prison and that the incident hurt him and his parents.**

A jury rejected Balbirona's first-degree robbery charge, believing his testimony that he didn't beat James M. Boreczky April 22 near a Sunset Beach bus stop about midnight. He said he only took Boreczky's suitcase.

But jurors convicted Balbirona's companion, Darrell Ortiz, 22, of second-degree robbery, rejecting Ortiz's story that he wasn't at the scene.

Simms also denied a defense request to release Balbirona on supervised release to his mother, but outlined bail conditions if his parents come up with $500 or 10 percent of the reduced bail.

She said he had to get enrolled in school to get his high school degree, submit to random drug testing and have no contact with the victim's family.

"If we don't get you now, we'll never get you," Simms said, asking Balbirona if he understood what she meant. He nodded.

Boreczky, 33, was visiting his brother on the North Shore when he cut short his visit and left for the airport.

He suffered multiple facial fractures, two black eyes, a broken nose and a broken jaw. He now has three metal plates to support his cheeks and was on medical leave for four months.

Deputy Prosecutor Maurice Arrisgado said the bail reduction was appropriate, but said he would ask for the maximum term of five years at sentencing.

He also said Balbirona's statement to Simms didn't acknowledge the impact of the incident to Boreczky.

"He wasn't trying to convey any remorse," he said. "He just didn't want to be a jailbird anymore."

Balbirona, who asked to make a statement, said that he didn't want to return to prison and that the incident hurt him and his parents.

"Please give me a second chance," he said, adding that he wanted to finish high school.

Keith Shigetomi, Balbirona's attorney, said in court that a Kahuku High School vice principal said Balbirona could return to class and likely graduate in June if he starts the spring semester.

He also said Balbirona has talked about entering the construction industry after getting his diploma.

Allen Balbirona, who said he dropped out of school in the eighth grade, said he wasn't raised by a father and didn't know how to be one. "I took away his daydreams," he said. "I was never a provider."

"But I'll do things differently. I will provide for him so he can prove himself."

Postal Customer Vol. 18, No. 7 • MidWeek Printing Inc., Honolulu, Hawaii • Suggested Subscription Price - $18/Year • 50¢ Per Vended Copy

MidWeek

Mailed To All Oahu Homes
Aug. 29, 2001

Hawaii's Favorite Newspaper

WIN $1,000!
Be our Mystery shopper!
Details inside.

'Easygoing' Judge Simms

Often maligned as too lenient, colleagues of Sandra Simms say critics lack all of the facts. 'Sentencing is the most important thing you do as a judge,' says Simms. 'You have to balance public safety with...whether a defendant can be productive.'

New Fines And Fees For False Alarms
Protecting your home may cost more under a proposed ordinance

Kamaaina Kangaroos
Content just to sit and chew, our wallabies may be disappearing, thanks to dogs, people and automobiles

FREAK DANCING: Banned At School, But Found All Over Town

Governor critical of rapist's light sentence

ASSOCIATED PRESS

Gov. Ben Cayetano yesterday said he's troubled by the probation sentence given to a convicted gang-rapist last week by an Oahu judge.

However, "I respect her right as a judge to make that kind of a call and that kind of a decision," he said.

Circuit Court Judge Sandra Simms released Habib Shabazz, 22, on probation after his mother and grandmother appealed for mercy. He had already spent 14 months in prison, awaiting trial and sentencing.

His co-defendant in the 1998 rape of a 17-year-old girl in a Waikiki hotel room, Mario Crawley, was sentenced to 10 years in prison. Simms ordered him to serve at least three years before being eligible for parole because he is a repeat offender.

After Shabazz's sentencing, the rape victim complained, saying she feels that she has been victimized again, this time by the court.

Cayetano said it's difficult to second-guess a judge without sitting through the trial.

"But the young man had 11 prior arrests and other kinds of problems and the offense being what it was, it seemed to me that (the sentence) was disproportionate to the crime," he said.

Those bothered by Simms' ruling can make their concerns known to the state's Judicial Selection Commission when Simms comes up for reappointment in four years, Cayetano said.

"I think Judge Simms will have to answer and be held accountable for her actions if and when she decides to apply for reappointment," he said.

It's not the first time Simms' actions have been criticized.

In 1998, Simms allowed a man convicted of viciously assaulting a 17-year-old boy in Makaha to remain free for three months before starting a 10-year prison term because his wife had given birth to their first child.

Last year, Simms allowed a 20-year-old man convicted of theft after the brutal beating of a vacationing Chicago police officer to remain on probation despite violating its terms.

Judge's son gets jail, fine for attack

Advertiser Staff

The 26-year-old son of a former state judge was ordered to spend eight days in jail and pay $975 in fines and fees in connection with what police said was an unprovoked attack on a teenager last year.

Circuit Judge Michael Wilson also ordered Richard H. Simms, son of former Circuit Judge Sandra Simms, to perform 100 hours of community service.

Richard Simms, a Mililani resident, pleaded guilty earlier to charges that included misdemeanor terroristic threatening and assault, driving without a license, drunken driving and second-degree theft related to the attack on a 17-year-old outside a Mililani restaurant Feb. 2.

When a passer-by stopped to help, Richard Simms stole the passer-by's car and later crashed it, prosecutors said.

Richard Simms asked the judge to defer accepting the guilty pleas to give him a chance to have the charges dropped. City prosecutors opposed that request, and the judge denied it. "I think it's a fair sentence," city deputy prosecutor Chris Van Marter said.

Sandra Simms submitted a letter in support of her son. Her request for a second 10-year term on the bench was rejected by the state Judicial Selection Commission last year.

H O N O L U L U
L I T E

By *Charles Memminger*
▲▲▲

Judge Simms setting new bench marks

TIME to dive into the Honolulu Lite Department of Fairness File. Today's subject: Circuit Judge Sandra Simms.

Only about a year ago prosecutors, letters to the editor writers and columnists were excoriating her honor for going too easy on criminals.

Among the exhibits:

➤ A man was convicted of punching and breaking the jaw of a 17-year-old boy while on probation for felony convictions. Simms let him stay out of prison for 3½ months so he could "bond" with his newborn son.

➤ Simms cut a 10-year prison sentence in half for a man convicted of drunken driving, his third drunken-driving conviction in a year.

➤ Imposed just a 30-day jail sentence on Rodney Balbirona, who violated his parole twice after being convicted of theft in connection with the brutal beating and robbery of a Chicago police officer on the North Shore.

Simms was quoted at the time as saying she was "utterly amazed" at the amount of misinformation the public had about the case.

She pointed out that Balbirona, while involved in the North Shore incident, had not been convicted of beating the victim and had no history of violence.

The public, unrestrained by such judicial hair-splitting, simply recognized Balbirona for what he was, an unrepentant punk who needed to be locked up for more than just 30 days.

I have to admit, I came down on the judge pretty hard, saying her track record of sparing the gavel and spoiling the defendant probably was going to result in even more mandatory minimum sentencing laws.

Update for Fairness File:

What a difference a year makes. You might say Judge Simms has turned over a new leaf but this is the Fairness File and we have to admit, we've never done an exhaustive review of her entire sentencing record. It's possible that her public sentence record was skewed by a few high-profile cases.

Simms has handed down a number of judgements recently that would make it hard to call her a complete softy now.

The biggest non-surprise for the public, however, would be Balbirona's complete betrayal of the Simms' leniency.

After blowing probation twice, Simms gave Balbirona a

D2 EDITORIALS

HONOLULU STAR-BULLETIN / SUNDAY, MAY 25

[OUR OPINION]

Remove state judges who abuse discretion

HAWAII has avoided the pitfalls of California and other states by continuing to allow judges discretion in sentencing criminals. While those states have required judges to impose automatic, punitive prison terms, Hawaii judges maintain some latitude in imposing sentences appropriate to the particular offender. When judges abuse that discretion, as Circuit Judge Sandra Simms did on numerous occasions, the judiciary should have a mechanism for expediently removing them from the bench.

Without comment, the Judicial Selection Commission has denied Simms' petition for a second 10-year term on the bench. Simms should have lost her robe years ago, but judges can be removed during their terms only for misconduct or disability. Those rules should be expanded to provide for removal after a judge has displayed a pattern of abuse of judicial discretion.

The Sentencing Project, a prison research and advocacy group, reports that nearly 10 percent of all inmates in state and federal prisons are serving life sentences, an 83 percent increase from 1992. In California and New York, almost 20 percent of the inmates

> ## THE ISSUE
>
> *State Circuit Judge Sandra Simms has been denied a second 10-year term on the bench by the Judicial Selection Commission.*

are serving life terms, at great taxpayer expense, because of laws aimed at getting tough on crime. Too many of those lifers are mentally ill, were convicted of drug crimes and property crimes or are women who killed their husbands after being battered by them.

Much of the harsher sentencing has resulted from mandatory minimum terms, truth-in-sentencing policies and the three-strikes law in California, which a Hawaii citizens panel wisely recommended against in January. Because of judicial discretion, only 6.9 percent of Hawaii's prison inmates have life terms, 2.5 percent less than the national average.

That discretion is jeopardized by judges like Simms.

Appointed to the Circuit Court bench in 1994 by then-Gov Cayetano, Simms showed up on the public radar in 1997 whe sentenced a 20-year-old man to probation — he already was probation from a previous crime — for stealing a Chicago po man's suitcase after the man's companion nearly beat the victioning officer to death on the North Shore. She later resente him to 30 days in jail after a public outcry. City Prosecutor P Carlisle cited the case in calling for an end to judicial discret and imposition of mandatory sentencing.

A year later, Simms postponed the six-month prison sente a professional boxer convicted of punching and breaking th of a 17-year-old boy at Makaha Beach so the boxer could ha to "bond" with his newborn son. "Having a child is a human experience," Simms remarked.

In recent years, Simms displayed an absurd degree of len in cases of companies and their clients claiming that the 18 throw of the Hawaiian kingdom was illegal, thus allowing th challenge state property titles and ignore state taxes. These simple cases of theft and tax evasion.

Verdict to unseat Simms was laudable

Mahalo to Sidney Ayabe, chairman of the Judicial Selection Commission, and other commissioners for not allowing Judge Sandra Simms another 10 years on the bench (Star-Bulletin, May 11). I have been amazed many times at the extreme leniency in sentencing or delay in incarceration of individuals convicted of violent and despicable crimes. My thought is that this decision was made not on the basis of race or gender, but because of her poor judgment and lack of concern for the safety of the community.

J.D. Nielsen
Honolulu

"LOOK AT 'EM! DISROBING AND HUMILIATING PRISONERS! ANIMALS!

[LETTERS TO THE EDITOR]

It's no shock that Simms did not get reappointed

IT IS WITH no joy and little surprise to learn that state Circuit Judge Sandra Simms will not be reappointed for another 10-year term on the bench.

I've been critical of Simms, but recent disclosures about her son's legal troubles seem to put some of Simms', shall we say, "charitable" treatment of criminals in perspective.

In a state in which judges are notoriously easy on bad guys (the general rule seems to be you have to kill at least TWO people to get life in prison — and then the governor might pardon you), Simms gave the term "softy" new meaning.

The most notorious of her get-outta-jail-free cards was dealt to a punk who took part in the brutal beating and robbery of a Chicago police officer on vacation on the North Shore. Rodney Balbirona was convicted of theft in that case be-

HONOLULU LITE

Charles Memminger

cause he simply stole the victim's belongings while his buddy beat the crapola out of the man. Simms found Balbirona's role in the robbery/beating exculpatory when the rest of the world considered him an equal partner in the near homi-

Please see Lite, D3

Lite: No joy, no surprise about Judge Simms

Continued from **D1**

cide. Simms gave Balbirona probation, which he violated. She gave him probation again, which he violated. And then, to the amazement of just about everyone, she gave him probation a THIRD time. He violated that, too. She finally put him in prison for five years.

Another guy already on probation for a felony broke a kid's jaw. Simms let him stay out of jail for nearly four months so he could bond with his newborn son, which he conveniently sired after the assault.

And, she cut a 10-year drunk-driving sentence in half for man convicted of DUI three times in one year.

Many, including then-Gov. Ben Cayetano, were hard pressed to understand Judge Simms' leniency, bizarre even by Hawaii standards.

Then this year, her 25-year-old son, Richard, was indicted for assault, terroristic threatening, DUI, leaving the scene of an accident and car theft after what can only be called a "hate crime." Richard Simms, who is black, assaulted a Caucasian 17-year-old without provocation, made racial slurs and fled in the victim's car, which he promptly crashed. Turns out Richard had a record of 15 prior arrests on charges including theft and DUI. Hmmm. Theft, DUI, assault ... sounds like the kinds of offenses Judge Mom went easy on.

Is it possible she saw a little of her son in those other defendants standing before her and reflexively gave them a break? I'm no psychologist, but it seems to me that her son's history might have had some bearing on her judicial demeanor, and at the very least, she should publicly have admitted to a conflict of interest.

The Judicial Selection Commission just rejected Simms' application for reappointment. There is no joy in seeing the judicial career of an obviously compassionate jurist come to an end, especially one who faces serious family problems. But there's love and there's tough love. Judge Simms should have practiced a bit more of the latter.

Epilogue

Going Home

Around the time I learned that my father had been admitted to the hospital, my court calendar was jammed. Like most judges, I presided over what is known as an individual calendar, which in essence means that when you are out of town, everything stops and waits for your return, but new cases are still added to your calendar on a weekly basis. I knew that the minute I returned to court the following morning, the chase would begin.

So, I told my youngest brother David that I would check back with him in the morning. The next day, when we spoke, my father was deteriorating rapidly. My staff, Susan and Sharon, began scrambling for a way to clear my court docket by calling attorneys and rescheduling hearings while I was figuring out what would happen to my son, Richard, and my husband, Hank, who was receiving on-going cancer treatment. Unfortunately, a grand jury had indicted him on felony charges stemming from a fight he had at a local bar. My husband Hank had been diagnosed with prostate cancer and was undergoing weekly treatments. On top of all this, the Judicial Selection Commission (JSC) who determine judicial retention applications, were deciding what to do with my pending reappointment to the first circuit court. What could possibly happen next?

My staff and I were on the phone constantly that day rescheduling my cases and getting updates from my brother. By Thursday, my brother called to say my father would be taken off life support. How did it get to this? What the hell had happened? A few hours later, Susan came into my chambers and stated simply, "Dad is gone." I could not move. I had only seen my Dad a few times within the last few years, yet I knew he took great pride in my legal career and judgeship. In addition, my children and the Hawai'i home we had nurtured for them, was the joy of his life. If there ever was a daughter who knew unconditional love, she was me. My dad loved me like no other, but now he was gone, and I did not even have chance to say good-bye. Within me was a horrible hurt.

I left for Chicago that same night. My daughter Sharon had left earlier that week. Hank obviously was too ill to travel and Richard was just not able to leave. Clearly, he had enough troubles of his own. At least, Richard could spend time with Hank. Our youngest daughter, Vera, was in Ann Arbor, completing her senior year at the University of Michigan. Thanks to her roommate, Chris, who drove her all the way to Chicago, Vera was able to join us the night before the services.

Since I arrived late in the day at O'Hare Airport, our family drove straight to Leak and Sons Funeral Home on Cottage Grove Avenue. John McCall, the funeral director and a long-time family friend, had already made all the funeral arrangements. John had known my parents all of his life because our parents had been close church friends for over fifty years.

Once I was at the funeral home, I instantly was surrounded by most of my cousins. They were waiting for me. They were as close to my parents as I was. Walter was there, as was Bob, Leonard, Laverne, Therese, Dolene and Ronald, Rod and Valerie, and my Aunt Daisy. Aunt Daisy, well in her 80s, was still impeccably dressed and cheerful. She and my father were as close as siblings because when my mother's brother Elmer died in 1958, leaving Aunt Daisy widowed with her two children Dolene and Rod, my parents were Aunt Daisy's "rock" of support. They shared every important moment in each other's lives— graduations, weddings, funerals, and holidays. My Aunt Daisy had even traveled with my parents to Hawai`i when I was first sworn in as a judge in 1991. Being in their midst was such a relief and a release, all I could do was fall into their arms.

For this reason, the funeral service was more like a loving family reunion than a truly somber occasion. But somehow, I still felt like a guest who had little to contribute. I had been away too long.

Chicago: The Apostolic Church of God

The Apostolic Church of God had been my Dad's life since it was founded by my grandfather Walter Clemons in the 1930s, so it just seemed fitting that he should be buried on his birthday at this house of worship. The church he called home for nearly all of his adult life is now a well-known mega church in Chicago's Woodlawn community with members in the thousands. It is the "place to be" for politicians and community leaders wanting to take the pulse of Chicago's Black gentry. But back in the 1940s when my Dad first arrived, the church was much smaller and tightly run by my grandfather.

Right up to his death, my father, remained a leader in the church's programs, chairing Sunday school, Deacon Board and the Board of Trustees. Not surprisingly, my parents' lives were centered within the programs and activities of the church and its organizations and affiliations. So many members of these various groups wanted to have their say at his service, and they did.

I watched and listened as countless church auxiliary groups came forward to read their resolutions of condolences reliving my father's life given to serving God. I did not personally know most of these members which reminded me how much the Church had grown from the early years when everyone knew everyone. Since I had been away for so long, I could see with fresher eyes the impact my father had on so many folks' lives. I was both at home and a stranger.

Now, what would be the family's roles in the services for my father? My middle brother, Raymond, is married to Jeannie who was the first woman to become an Assistant Pastor at the Apostolic Church of God. We had grown up together as kids. Who better than Jeannie and John McCall could arrange the funeral services for my father? Ray would direct the Sanctuary Choir. David, and his wife Claudia, would be the contact point for the nieces, nephews, cousins, and family. Their home would be the gathering place. And, somewhere someone said, "Sandra? She'll represent us. She will speak for us." At the time, I remember thinking, what do I know. I wasn't even here for my father.

Lawyers usually are not short for words, regardless of the circumstances. And me? Well, I usually summon up something appropriate, effective, and even quickly. But, not this time. I just couldn't think straight, nor could I tell anyone that I couldn't. I just couldn't. A fiercely lit torch was passing and suddenly I, Sandra, the eldest in our family, had become the parent my parents had been before me. Was I even up to the task?

Homecoming

As I looked around at my father's grandchildren, nephews and nieces gathered in this beautiful place of worship, I began to realize that it was no longer about me. I had to become for them what my father was to me. So, rather than remain without a voice, I decided that my role would be as MC, introducing the children to the congregation like David, Jr., lawyer; Dayna Lynn, singer; Sharon, first born and speaker; Vera, mom's namesake engineer and athlete. Then we had his favorite niece, Louisa, the youngest daughter of his youngest brother, Jimmy, who had preceded my dad in death. "Puff," as he always called her, was now a DuPage county prosecutor.

On April 5, 2004, hundreds and hundreds of people attended the funeral service for Gerald Raymond Nuckolls Senior, my father. They steadily streamed past our family, to pay their respects and to share their condolences and memories with me. In some ways, it was like watching the past flow into life. I was seeing so many faces I had not seen in years, even family members from whom I'd felt out of touch. For example Aunt Louise and Aunt Kathryn, my Dad's sisters, were the Bloomington group in Central Illinois who we would visit as children during the summers.

Now I'm smiling through tears as I greet my childhood friends, Jan and Paula from Grand Rapids, Michigan. I'm so happy to see them. In our teens, we spent many weekends on the "church circuit" traveling and singing with our respective church choirs on weekends at churches around the Midwest: Cleveland, Columbus, Indianapolis, and Detroit. We were in each other's weddings, our closets were lined with bridesmaid's dresses and matching shoes, but I hadn't seen these friends in over 20 years. I had been away for a long time.

Their father, the late Bishop William Abney, was the pastor of a large church in Grand Rapids, and was my father's friend for decades. Our parents had been staunch fixtures in the Pentecostal Assemblies of the World. Bishop Abney was approaching his eighties, but his trademark tenor voice was still strong as he sang for my father: "God has been good to me, I can't complain." I couldn't either.

A steady stream of hands and hugs grasped me. As I caught more and more familiar faces, I just could not stop crying as the memories flooded back. Here now are Tom and Sara Olesker. Tom's father owned the clothing store that my father worked in for all of his adult life. Every Christmas Eve Tom's father brought us children tons of toys, even though they were Jewish.

Here is Marge Clemons who has the most beautiful soprano voice, and who sang at my wedding ceremony. She was the only other size 3 I knew, besides me, once upon a time. Marge is hugging me. Over Marge's head I see Betty McDaniel who worked at Catholic Charities. In the early days, Betty arranged summer jobs for all the teens, and taught me how to model when "Black became Beautiful" in 1968.

As Betty walks away, William and Vivian Nelson crush me in a group bear hug. I'm overwhelmed with joy and sorrow. I met Vivian when I was 15 and she'd just come to Chicago from Alabama. She worked at Catholic Charities with Toni Moore and me. Toni would later become my stepsister when my father married her mother, Wilhelmenia. We loved to sew and honed our seamstress skills to the point where we were mastering Vogue patterns. Toni and Vivian would progress in their seamstress training to become "skilled." I, on the other hand, had stopped sewing years ago, just as I had stopped visiting my hometown friends. I've been away for so long.

The late Bishop Brazier's eulogy for my father was enlightening and intimate. He and my dad had been friends for over 50 years, so you could feel the bishop's pain as he shared their times together. Resplendent in his ecclesiastic robes, he recalled that their friendship had begun in World War II, in the segregated army where Negro soldiers were second-class to even white Nazi prisoners on trains that rode through the southern states. The details of the indignities they endured to prepare us for this time of change and opportunity were seldom discussed by the men of my dad's generation. I think they omitted many of the sordid details, in part, to prepare and secure the path for the next generation, by shielding us from some of the pain they endured, so we could focus on the tasks before us.

At one point, Bishop Brazier even noted, that in all the years he had been pastor, he had never made a major decision about the church without seeking my dad's counsel. Their trust and loyalty to each other is a story in and of itself. When I visited the church a few years ago, the desk and cubicle where my father used to sit, was still vacant. The Bishop told me that he could not bring himself to allow someone else to sit there. He was hurting as much as the family because he was family.

After the eulogy, I made a powerful connection with an attractive, gentle woman named Gracie Prater. I had never met her before, and knew almost nothing about her. However, both my brothers had told me she always took care of my father on the Sundays he'd stay at church from morning until the last service was over. I learned that Gracie often would ensure that my father ate his meals properly, and in later years, would send him home when he did not seem well. This could be a challenge sometimes, because my father was so dedicated to the church and was usually among the last to leave. At the gravesite, she gently took my arm and told me now she would take care of me. I don't know if my tears flowed from joy, sorrow or a comingling of both emotions.

Gracie was as good as her word. At the funeral, when I could not hold back my tears, she silently slipped me a tissue. Since I left my coat in the funeral car, she wrapped me up in her sweet-smelling fur coat when the wind blew. Throughout my father's service, she held my hand and hugged me whenever she thought I needed comfort, which was often. Gracie was there the whole day for me, just for me, solely because I was my father's daughter. I will never forget her.

For me, this was a tough, emotional day, brimming with joys and intense sadness. Yet, in my shifting moments of surreal pleasure and fearful isolation, I felt myself becoming stronger, like my father. This day's events reminded me of the powerful legacy I'd had to build on all these years.

"Talking Story" about Dad

As is customary in our family and culture's funeral tradition, we gathered at my brother, David's house, just down the street from the church. It's a new neighborhood of gentrified homes along 63rd

Street, a street once ruled by the Blackstone Rangers gang and ravaged raw by its violence. This street is now almost idyllic with neat lawns fronting the red-bricked fancy homes. The interiors of the houses are spacious and elegant, and my brother and his wife share their home generously with friends and family, which is exactly how we were raised.

In my parent's apartment on Paxton Avenue, there was a large oak table in the dining room where we would all gather while my father told deliciously detailed stories about everybody and everything! Now David and Claudia's family room takes the place of my parents' table. Everyone gathers here for games, meals and more stories. Somehow, these stories compete successfully with the ear-splitting din of the huge flat-screen TV fixated on ESPN, or whatever Chicago team is playing whatever sport at a given moment.

On the day of Dad's service, David and Claudia's family room was filled with steaming plates of homemade food: honey-cured hams, platters of fried chicken, creamy casseroles of macaroni and cheese, yellow potato salads, golden sweet yams, spicy collard and mustard greens, colorful veggie salads for the health conscious, and a huge array of every delectable sinful dessert known to a baker. And folks just kept arriving with fresh bowls and plates of good food.

In honor of my father, the consummate story-teller, people began sharing their stories about my parents as all of us heaped our plates with mouth-watering delicacies. As the Hawaiians would say, we began to "talk story."

Bishop Vanuel Little and his wife, Alice, were first among the storytellers. They pastor a large church in Oklahoma City but met at the Apostolic Church of God through my grandfather. Bishop Little recalled how he had come to Chicago as a starry- eyed young single man, just like my father. People told him and many others to find "Elder Clemons" when they got to Chicago. Family members on the church circuits told them that Elder Clemons would help them find a place to stay, find a job, and, of course, a place to worship. And, my father did.

Many of the folks at David and Claudia's house also talked story about the days and times at "57th and Wabash." In the middle of this block, my grandfather owned a large apartment building where our families lived, and where so many others simply showed up and rang the doorbell looking for "Elder Clemons." My parents' apartment was across the hall from my grandparents' on the first floor of the building. That means ours was the first apartment you would encounter once you entered the vestibule. Since visitors had to be "buzzed" in by ringing the doorbell next to the name of the family you were visiting, we could always hear the doorbell buzz for every visitor who came. Clearly, most visitors came to see my grandfather.

When my grandfather, the oldest of 15 siblings, moved to Chicago from Georgia in the 1920's with the Negro Migration of that time, several of his brothers and sisters migrated with him. Therefore, almost everyone living in grandfather's building was related. Fortunately, this property was a lovely, spacious three story building with six large apartments and two basement "studios." In this space we experienced a continuous flow of colorful characters who would show up to begin new lives in Chicago, or just pass through on their way somewhere else. Before voice mail, mobile phones and text messages, people would just drop by and hope to find you at home. So, in the small towns and communities from where these Black folk migrated, the word was to "go see Elder Clemons when you get to Chicago."

When he traveled to preach at little churches in the Midwest, driving his big, black Buick Roadmaster, with his grandsons in tow, Elder Clemons, or grandpa, was somewhat of a celebrity—the "big-time" preacher from the city. And, of course, during those times, since African Americans on the road could not stay in any hotels, there was an underground lodging network which my grandfather was a part of it. He was never turned away from a clean bed nor a hot meal, and to my knowledge, he never turned anybody away who came to him.

My father also came to Chicago to get away from Bloomington, his home town in central Illinois. It could just as easily have been in the heart of Mississippi. Bloomington is still home to several well-known universities: Illinois Wesleyan, Illinois State Teachers College, nearby Bradley University, and Western Illinois, none of which would admit "Negro" students when my dad was young. The town's largest department store, Livingston's,' did not allow "Negroes" in to shop, nor could you eat in the front of "Steak and Shake," but you could pick up food in the back and take it home. Perhaps, there weren't enough Black people in the town to warrant establishing an entire segregated public school system, so the few Blacks who lived in Bloomington were educated in integrated public schools, but only up to high school, my dad among them.

Fortunately, my dad learned his father's trade of tailoring, in the shop attached to their home. Both men were excellent tailors, as were my aunts. Not surprisingly, my childhood memories of my grandparents project them as "larger than life." I recall that people seemed to be always around them, especially when my grandparents presided over huge, savory meals! Even at breakfast, there would be ten people sitting at our table.

We kept live chickens in a coop under the back porch until the city declared the keeping of live poultry illegal. Nevertheless, our families always had good, fresh meats. That was because in addition to being a minister, my grandfather brokered workers for the stockyards. In those days, Chicago had the largest stockyard in the country, since the cattle trains from the west literally ended in Chicago. And, on hot summer days, when the cows were being trucked to the stockyards on 43rd Street down State Street (one block over from Wabash), the cloying stench lingered for days. My grandfather thought nothing of rounding up a group of guys at the neighborhood tavern, putting them to work in the smelly stockyards, and then bringing them home to have a meal with his family, on the good china, no less! But this was the world in which I was raised, where supporting others and helping wherever you could and was just a way of life.

Going Home

I am a part of my father and my mother. I am that; they are me. The painful but glorious funeral was a colorful parade of faces, memories, tears joy, and sorrow, and celebration for the life of the man who gave me life and loved me all the time. I saw familiar faces evoking familiar memories and new faces with still familiar memories, my past and my future.

I had begun the day feeling almost like a stranger who was far removed from her life and surroundings. But, as I began to embrace and absorb all the events that had transpired during this emotion-filled day, I had a new realization, a new understanding of myself. These were the people and lives that made up the core of my being. My faith, my strength, my compassion came from this place. I was overcome with gratitude.

After my father's funeral, I was in a place of grace, but I had little time to mourn his loss, or celebrate my new-found faith because my interview with the JSC was the first item on the agenda when I returned to Honolulu. Secretly, I was pleased I had not been in town for all the swirling speculation and gossiping that had surely taken place in my absence.

When I walked into the room, I took a seat as directed, facing the commissioners who were seated around an oblong table, with copies of my large dossier in front of them. Some smiled, some didn't. A few members of the committee even looked away, but I felt strangely and wonderfully at peace. I felt the arms of my father and grandfather embracing me with loving support. Nothing else mattered, even the fact that my life on that particular bench was over.

So, I returned to Hawai`i, to the island of Oahu, or the "gathering place," after the funeral to face a multitude of challenges, personal and professional. Yet finally, I felt the surging power of my inner strength, my moral convictions, my deep spirituality, and my loving, supportive family, both on this island and on the mainland. Their strength combined with mine, is what I have come to rely upon. Finally, after so many years of professional and personal service, I was going home to my own gathering place, carrying lessons from the bench; objectivity, justice, service, gratitude and aloha.

About The Author

SANDRA ARLENE SIMMS

RETIRED. CIRCUIT COURT JUDGE, STATE OF HAWAI`I
MEDIATOR/ARBITRATOR
ADJUNCT LECTURER IN CRIMINAL JUSTICE,
CHAMINADE UNIVERSITY

Judge Sandra Simms was appointed to the First Circuit Court, Twelfth Division in May 1994. Prior to her appointment to the Circuit Court, she served on the District Court from November 1991. She retired from the bench June 1, 2004.

Judge Simms was born in Chicago, Illinois. She is a graduate of Hyde Park High School, and obtained a B. A. from the University of Illinois, Chicago with a major in Sociology and Political Science. She earned her Juris Doctor degree from DePaul University, College of Law in 1978.

After graduating from the University of Illinois, she was employed as a flight attendant for United Airlines from 1972-1977. She and her husband Hank, moved to Hawai`i in 1979 upon his transfer with United Airlines. From 1980 until March 1982, she was law clerk to the Honorable Yoshimi Hayashi, then Chief Judge for the then newly formed Intermediate Court of Appeals.

She served as Deputy Corporation Counsel for the City and County of Honolulu from 1982 until 1991. In that capacity, she served as legal counsel to a variety of city agencies and commissions, including, the Police Commission, Civil Service Commission, Liquor Commission, Building, Public Works, Fire Department, and Family Support Division. She also served as a Staff Attorney for the Department of the Attorney General's Office of Information Practices until she was appointed by Chief Justice Herman Lum to the District Court of the First Circuit, in November, 1991, becoming the first African American female judge in the state of Hawai`i. In May 1994, Governor John Waihee appointed her to the position of Circuit Court Judge for the

First Judicial Circuit, State of Hawai`i. As a trial judge, she presided over matters involving domestic violence, restraining orders, civil proceedings and felony jury trials, a substantial number of which were extensively covered by the media.

She is a member of the distinguished panel of neutrals for Dispute Prevention Resolution, a private alternative dispute resolution firm in Honolulu, and the Supreme Court's Appellate Mediation Conference. She has completed mediation training at Center for ADR in Honolulu and the Strauss Institute at Pepperdine University.

Most recently, she was named Adjunct Lecturer in Criminal Justice Studies at Chaminade University in Honolulu.

She served on a number of judicial committees, contributing to the work of the Jury Innovations Committee, the Domestic Violence Backlog Reduction Project, and the District Court Civil Rules Committee among others.

She was a member of the Judiciary's Speakers Bureau, and gave numerous presentations to a variety of community organizations, schools and forums to assist them in understanding the judicial system. Among the programs she has participated in have been school career days, The Peoples' Law School, Hawai`i High School Mock Trial Tournament, William S. Richardson Law School Appellate Advocacy, and the Dr. Martin Luther King , Jr. Coalition,

She has been a speaker and/ or presenter for innumerable community organizations and functions, including: The Rotary Club, Chaminade University, Soroptimist International, NAACP, Delta Sigma Theta Sorority, Honolulu Black Nurses, Trinity Missionary Baptist Church, University of Hawai`i SEED program, Sacred Hearts Academy, Honolulu Masons, Hawai`i Chapter of The Links, Inc., YWCA Leadership Luncheon, and The Girl Scout Council and various military programs and forums.

Judge Simms is a member of The National Bar Association, The American Bar Association and is a past president of the Afro American Lawyers Association. She currently serves on the Hawai`i State Board of Bar Examiners.Active with the Judicial Council of the National Bar Association; she has also served as a group facilitator for the

National Judicial College in Reno, Nevada.

Her community and civic association include six years of service on Neighborhood Board #25 (1983-1990), and on various public school committees where her children attended.

She is an active member and past president of Soroptimist International Waikīkī Foundation, Inc – an international professional service organization that works to improve the lives of women and girls.

She is Vice President for Mental Health America of Hawai`i (formerly the Mental Health Association in Hawai`i) and coordinates its successful annual Mahalo Awards Luncheon.

She is a long time member, past Area Officer and past President of the Hawai`i Chapter of The Links, Incorporated, a national women's service organization that focuses on cultural and community enrichment programs for and about African Americans.

A student and admirer of Hawaiian quilting, she is also a member of Sewjourner Truth, a group of attorneys and judges who enjoy the art of quilting.